WHATNOT

WHATNOT

A Compendium of Victorian Crafts & Other Matters

• •

Being a compilation of Authentic Home & Hand Crafts
popular in the era of
Her Most Excellent Majesty, VICTORIA, by the Grace of God Queen,
assembled from the original 19th century edition of
CASSELL'S HOUSEHOLD GUIDE, London,
and enlarged and expounded by the present authors

MARJORIE HENDERSON

and

ELIZABETH WILKINSON

Together with sundry offerings on Victorian Life & Manners
arranged & made suitable for the entertainment & edification of
Gentlewomen and Gentlemen Readers
of all pursuits and persuasion,

• •

and published by

WILLIAM MORROW AND COMPANY, INC.
New York

Library of Congress Catalog Card Number 76-11715

ISBN 0-688-03155-2
1 2 3 4 5 6 7 8 9 10

This book was developed and prepared for publication under the
direction of James and Carolyn Robertson at The Yolla Bolly Press,
Covelo, California, during the fall and winter months of 1976-77.
Staff: Sharon Miley, Gene Floyd, Harris Dienstfrey, Jay Stewart,
Jane Dienstfrey, and Jim Thomas.

The Authors' Appreciation Is Extended to:

The Victoria and Albert Museum, London, for permission to reproduce
the photographs that appear on the cover and pages 16, 44, 223.

Msrs. Cassell, Petter & Galpin, London, publishers of
Cassell's Household Guide, 1877.

For MILDRED ROBSON, whose
library was the source of this book,
and for LOU WILKINSON, who
lived in the workshop.

Table of Contents

PART ONE

MOSTLY DOMESTIC ARTS

Introduction   17

An Evening Party in the Manner of the 1870s: *A Cold*   18
    Collation, Decorations, Recipes, Parlor Games and Forfeits

Temporary Decorations for an Impromptu Ballroom   29

Principles of Good Taste in Household Furnishings   34

The General Servant   36

Active Recreations for Ladies: *Riding, Calisthenics, Archery,*   38
    Sea Bathing, Bagatelle, Croquet, Ice Skating

PART TWO

HOUSEHOLD DECORATIVE ARTS

Introduction   45

Imitation Ebony and Ivory Chessboard   48

Decorative Shellwork: *Shell Box, Shell Flowers*   52

Glass Decoration in Imitation Marble   63

Embossing on Glass   64

Potichomanie: *Potiche*   67

Ornamental Jardinières: *Imitation Sèvres China and Wedg-*   68
    wood, Natural Flowerpot Covers, Flowerpot Stands,
    Etrusco-Egyptian Flowerpots, Cardboard Fretwork Covers

Point Lace Work: *Designs for a Sofa Cushion*   72

Point Lace Paper Fly Cages   77

Beadwork: *Bead Mosaic, Beadwork on Wire*   79

Furniture Decorated with Chintz   82

Leafwork on Furniture: *Leafwork Desk*   86

Chinese Album   90

Bookbinding: *Scrapbook, Designs for an Album Frontispiece or Cover*   92

Ornamental Buttonwork: *Teapot Cosies, Egg Baskets, Mats*   94

Black and Gilded Box   99

The Art and Application of Illumination: *Illuminated Backgammon Board*   103

Monograms and Cyphers   111

Articles for Gifts and Fancy Fairs: *Turkish Slipper, Guitar, Mandoline, Fish Pincushion, Hand Penwiper, Bellows*   114

Work-Box Furniture: *Pole Screens, Chair, Loo Table*   117

Fans: *Feather Fan, Bouquet Fan*   119

Paper Flower Making: *Cabbage Rose, Half-Blown Rosebud, Stamens and Pistils, Carnation, Fuchsia, Daisies, Poppy*   124

Summer Dressings for Fireplaces: *Simple Fire Paper, Shredded Tarlatan with Myrtle Wreath, Rustic Fender*   129

Ornamental Spills   132

Fish-Scale Embroidery   133

D'oyleys from Natural Foliage   135

Conework: *Conework Basket, Conework Pincushion*   137

Imitation Coral Ornaments: *Imitation Coral Vase, Imitation Coral Basket, Table Ornaments*   140

Souvenirs and Tasteful Trifles: *Gentleman's Toilette Case, Spectacle Case, Lady's Shoe Tidy, Decorated Needle-Book, Music Wrappers, Key Bag*   144

Working in Hair: *Hair Brooches, Sentimental Ornament*   149

Colored Transparencies   154

Watercolor Drawing on Wood: *Salad Servers, Bonbonnières*   155

Skeleton Leaves   160

The Water Bouquet   162

Picture Checkerboards: *Children's Checkerboard*   164

Scrapscreen   168

Easter Eggs   173

Christmas Decorations: *Decorating the House, Decorating the Tree*   175

PART THREE
IN THE GARDEN

Introduction   187

Rockwork and Grottoes   189

An Aeolian Harp   192

Rustic Garden Furniture: *Rustic Settee for a Doll*   193

Flower Containers: *Rustic Hanging Baskets, Plant Stand, Fancy Work with Acorns*   199

Summer Houses   204

Fern Cases: *Hexagonal Rustic Fern Case*   207

Floral Ornaments for Windows and Back Yards: *Window Canopy, Temporary Arbor, Portable Screen of Ivy*   212

Tame Pigeons and Dovecots   215

Sun Dials: *Carved Redwood Horizontal Sun Dial*   217

Photographs of Crafts

Tipsy Cake and Syllabubs	21	Bouquet Fan	121
Chessboard	49	Imitation Coral Ornament	141
Shell Box	53	Sentimental Ornament	151
Shell Flowers	60	Bonbonnière	157
Embossing on Glass	65	Children's Checkerboard	165
Furniture Decorated with Chintz	83	Scrapscreen	169
Leafwork on Furniture	87	Rustic Furniture	195
Buttonwork	95	Acorn Hanging Basket	201
Black and Gilded Box	101	Fern Case	209
Backgammon Board	107		

Introduction

T ALL STARTED when we discovered, in a family collection, the four volumes of *Cassell's Household Guide,* published in London in 1875. We sat for an afternoon, each with a book, interrupting each other with "Listen to this " and "Wouldn't this be fun to make!" We were amused and enchanted with the text's unexpected and often unintentional flashes of humor, the florid vocabulary, and the delightful illustrations.

These books were written primarily for a burgeoning middle class whose newly acquired prosperity had created among its members a need for education in the finer points of social usage, the management of home and servants, and the intricacies of "good taste." The ladies of these households now had the leisure to concern themselves with the decoration of their homes and gardens, and to learn the arts and crafts that were considered the necessary accomplishments of their position.

The author gave practical advice on subjects ranging from "Dancing the Cotillion" to "Management of Household Drains," and the more we read, the more fascinated we became with the Victorian scene. Each page revealed a new and intriguing dichotomy of prudery and earthiness; in one instance the *Household Guide* has our dainty Victorian lady digging the brains out of a bird's skull to make a fire screen, and in the next, writing sentimental verses in a cherub-decked album.

It was the *Household Guide's* wealth of designs and instructions for craft projects that really held our attention. Victorians, like nature, abhorred a vacuum, and delighted in filling up every vacant space: a blank on the wall, an empty spot on the table, or an unembellished piece of furniture. It has been said that only the Grecians could have produced the Venus de Milo, and only the Victorians could have thought of putting a clock in her stomach! They, with great enthusiasm, vitality, and tremendous self-confidence, borrowed from every period of design and from every culture, added their own touches and created some marvelous, mad things. This was much too interesting to keep to ourselves and so this book was born.

With so much irresistible material, our biggest dilemma in compiling a book lay in deciding what not to include. After much sifting, sorting, and experimenting, what we have finally evolved is a book of Victorian hand, home, and garden crafts, the great majority of which we have done ourselves. In many cases the techniques have been completely altered for practicability—without, we trust, losing too much of their authenticity and charm. Other material has been included because it was amusing or informative and projected that essential flavor that so captivated us on first reading the *Household Guide*.

However you use this book—as a careful guide to reproducing the crafts in it, as a takeoff point for designing your own bits of Victoriana, or even as a small window into the past—we hope you will have as good a time with it as we had writing it. If you find that your vocabulary becomes a trifle overblown and your sentence structure contains too many parenthetical phrases and your friends think you're getting a little queer in the attic, just tell them it's Cassell's Syndrome and that it will pass.

WHATNOT

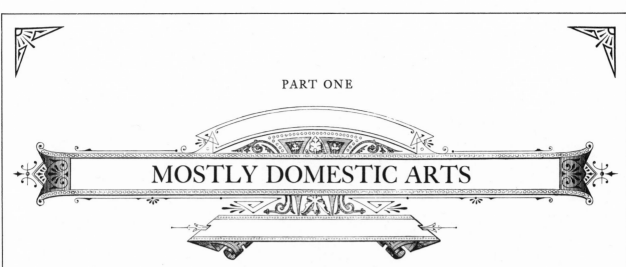

PART ONE

MOSTLY DOMESTIC ARTS

An Evening Party in the Manner of the 1870s

Decorating an Impromptu Ballroom

Principles of Good Taste in Furnishings

The General Servant

Active Recreations for Ladies

Introduction

ARCHERY, bathing costumes, and a dinner party may seem odd subjects to begin a book on crafts, but let us explain. Having spent almost a year immersed in *Cassell's Household Guide*, making bodkin cases and syllabubs, potichomanie and spills, these objects and terms ceased to belong to the half-remembered world of grandmothers and great-grandmothers, and became in measure, part of our world. Our purpose here, then, is to provide a background sampler of the Victorian woman's pursuits—the household concerns and opinions that shaped her decorative tastes, the active recreations considered suitable for her, and the type of entertaining she might have done. We hope to evoke the atmosphere that will enhance for you (as it did for us) the value and charm of the crafts that were so much a part of this fascinating era.

An Evening Party in the Manner of the 1870s

A Cold Collation

The preparation and serving of elegant repasts was a major preoccupation of the Victorians. In fact, so much of the *Household Guide* was devoted to these highly important and very tempting subjects that we decided we simply had to entertain our friends and families at Christmas by giving a dinner party in the Victorian manner, complete with costumes, menu, decorations, and parlor games. But where to start?

Cassell describes dinner parties ranging from the extremely formal with twenty removes and requiring a servant for every two guests, to an impromptu supper for eight for which "seven dishes at least are to be pre-

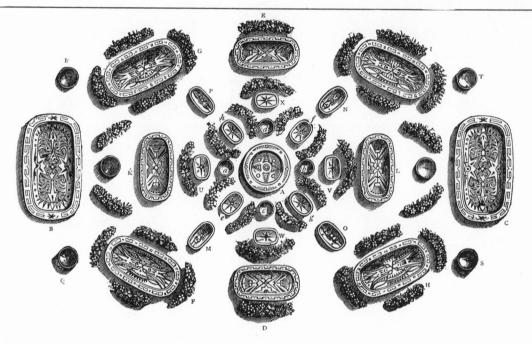

CASSELL'S TABLE DESIGN AND MENU FOR A SIMPLE COLD COLLATION

A. Glass stand for flowers.
B. Soup — white, Julienne, or mullagatawny.
C. Cold fowls, cut up; only wings, breasts, and merrythoughts on a dish garnished with flowers, parsley, beetroot, lemon, &c.
D. Game, cold pheasants, garnished.
E. Game, cold partridge, garnished.
F. Oyster patties.
G. Lark patties.
H. Pate de lievre.
I. Eel patties.
K. Potatoe soufflees.
L. Lobster salad.
M. Tongue, glazed and garnished.
N. Ham in thin slices.
O. Oeufs a la neige.
P. Collared meat, glazed and garnished with savory jelly.

Q. Ham sandwiches.
R. Anchovy sandwiches.
S. Potted lobster sandwiches.
T. Tongue sandwiches.
U. Cake in mould.
V. Wafers.
W. Galette — French cake.
X. Rout cakes.
a. Lemon jelly.
b. Orange jelly.
c. Lemon jelly.
d. Raspberry jelly.
e. Fresh or preserved fruits.
f. Fresh or preserved fruits.
g. Fresh or preserved fruits.
h. Fresh or preserved fruits.

pared.'' Which dishes? Cassell offers this heart-burning dialogue, in which the hostess addresses the cook as follows: ''What have you in the larder?'' The probable answer will be, 'Cold fowl, ham, tongue, game, and cold roast meat.' ''These will do very well, with a few lighter viands and sweets to make up.''

These remarks will give you a partial picture of the ample nature of Victorian cuisine. The more elaborate dinners, one feels, would put to shame a state dinner at the White House. How could we begin to re-create even an impromptu supper that was true to the period?

We regretfully decided that a proper sit-down dinner was somewhat beyond our combined household staffs (all two of us) and so were delighted to find the following comments on entertaining at a cold collation.

A very agreeable entertainment is the unceremonious repast which, whether called a déjeuner, a luncheon, a meat-tea, or a cold collation, is the same in principle and composition. It is something of a very elastic nature and may contain as few things as you please, provided there be plenty to eat and drink, or it may be a collection of rarities got together from the uttermost ends of the world. Although the meal is essentially a cold one, a few hot things may be interspersed.

In giving a hot dinner, a mountain of victuals is the height of vulgarity and bad taste. There is only one thing worse than putting too much upon a table — if it be worse — and that is too little. But in a cold dinner, the whole of it being presented at once, the weakness of making a show may be indulged in without incurring the blame of ostentatious profusion. Of course it increases the interest of the display, when there are means of using articles of plate, china and glass, which are in themselves curiosities or objects of art.

The suggestions for a cold collation lent themselves very well to a buffet dinner for thirty-five people. Our menu was a simplified version of the one given by Cassell, and by using all of our own silver serving dishes and borrowing many others, we managed to re-create the table arrangement with a satisfyingly ostentatious display!

Decorations

The decorations for our dinner party centered on two things: the Victorian Christmas tree (a full description, with designs for ornaments, begins on page 176) and the buffet table itself. We arranged the dishes on the table following Cassell's plan, but substituted holly for the flower garlands illustrated in the *Household Guide*. We sighed longingly for a Flora (Fig. 1), or Exhibition (Fig. 2) vase to use as a table decoration, but found it easier, and just as dramatic, to duplicate the "Old fashioned centerpiece, a pyramid of glass salvers, laden with jellies, creams, syllabubs, custards, and crowned with a Tipsy Cake" (we'll get to syllabubs and tipsy cakes shortly). We used three round silver trays, in graduated sizes. The largest tray formed the base, a silver wine cooler supported the middle tray, and a slender silver vase held up the smallest tray where the Tipsy Cake Hedgehog, ringed with holly, reposed in festive splendor! (A note of caution here: Be very sure your trays are well balanced so the whole construction doesn't collapse if someone knocks against the table.) We filled the wine cooler with ice to help keep the desserts chilled during dinner.

FIG. 1

FIG. 2

Our Menu:

Shrimp Vinaigrette
Cold Baked Ham
Cold Roast Beef
Cold Roast Turkey

Hot Chestnut Dressing   Cauliflower Mousse

Molded Cucumber Salad   Salmagundi

Ginger Chutney
Raw Cranberry & Orange Relish
Horseradish Sauce

Hot Buttered Bisquits

Sweet Jellies   Tipsy Cake   Syllabubs

Claret Cup   Fruit Punch
Coffee

Recipes

We wanted to keep the foods we served for our cold collation as authentic as possible, but found most of Cassell's recipes too indefinite about measurements to use and, because this is a craft, not a cook-book, we felt it outside our purpose to experiment with them (with two exceptions: Syllabubs and Claret Cup sounded so much better than others we had tried, we did work out measurements for them). In many of the recipes however, it is the *arrangement* of the food that is the most Victorian part of the dish, as you will see in the recipes for Salmagundi, Tipsy Cake, and Lobster Salad, where we generally followed Cassell. For the other dishes in our menu we used our own favorite family recipes that were most similar to those in the *Household Guide*.

SALMAGUNDI

Select your ingredients for their contrast of hue as well as of flavor — green parsley, brown herring or anchovy, yellow yolks, white of egg, pink veal, scarlet hung beef, &c., all minced to different degrees of fineness. Take

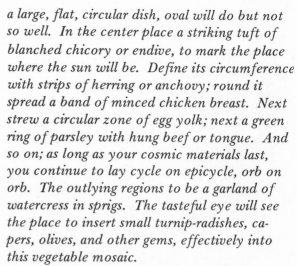

a large, flat, circular dish, oval will do but not so well. In the center place a striking tuft of blanched chicory or endive, to mark the place where the sun will be. Define its circumference with strips of herring or anchovy; round it spread a band of minced chicken breast. Next strew a circular zone of egg yolk; next a green ring of parsley with hung beef or tongue. And so on; as long as your cosmic materials last, you continue to lay cycle on epicycle, orb on orb. The outlying regions to be a garland of watercress in sprigs. The tasteful eye will see the place to insert small turnip-radishes, capers, olives, and other gems, effectively into this vegetable mosaic.

Since we were serving several cold meats separately, our salmagundi consisted of carrot and celery sticks, sprigs of broccoli, olives, pickled mushrooms, radishes, deviled eggs, anchovies, green onions, etc. with a bowl of dip for the "sun."

TIPSY CAKE

Procure a mould the shape of a hedgehog or a porcupine [we used a melon mould]*; in this make a sponge cake. When cold, set in a hollow glass dish. . . . Pour over the back of the porcupine, to soften it, a glass of Marsala, Madeira, or other wholesome wine. Then stick the back full of* [slivered] *almonds, to represent quills, and make the eyes with currents or raisins* [and a nose with a maraschino cherry]*. When wanted, pour round it, in the hollow of the dish, as much of the same wine as it will soak without melting or falling to pieces. Some add brandy to the wine, but that is apt to make it a little too tipsy. If you wish, on the contrary, to render it milder, when you judge that a sufficient quantity of wine has been absorbed by the cake, fill up the hollow of the dish with whipped cream or some kind of custard.*

We especially recommend the following recipe; it has become one of our favorite gala desserts. We serve it in parfait glasses or champagne flutes. On a recent visit to England, we found that syllabubs are still frequently served, and we ordered them whenever they appeared on a menu. But we never found a

An old-fashioned centerpiece: a pyramid of salvers laden with jellies, creams, syllabubs, custards, and crowned with a tipsy cake in the form of a hedgehog.

syllabub as light and delectable as one made from this recipe.

SYLLABUBS

Makes 12 servings.

Flavor a pint of Madeira with two or three drops of orange flower water; or you may steep it overnight with the rind of lemon cut very thin. Put it into a large bowl. Sweeten it liberally [with ¾ cup sugar, or to taste] ; *stir in three tablespoons of brandy, the juice of a lemon, and a pint and a half of the richest* [whipping] *cream. If you want the froth of your Syllabubs to be very stiff, add the white of an egg. Then beat all to a froth with your osier whisk* [an electric beater is faster and more efficient] . *As the froth rises, skim it off with a spoon and with it fill your syllabub glasses, heaping it as high as it will hold together; and so on, till your cream is all whipped up.* [This is more easily done by two people, one holding the beater and the other skimming.] *Set the Syllabubs in a cool place; they will get firm and settle into a highly flavored liquor, capped by a crown of snowy froth. When half of your glasses are filled with white Syllabub, you may vary the color of the rest and make them pink by mixing the remainder of the cream with a little red currant or raspberry jelly melted.*

CLARET CUP

Makes 24 servings.

Into a half gallon of claret in a large jug, pour one cup of brandy. Add an orange and a lemon, both thinly sliced. Let stand for half an hour or more; and before using pour in one quart of iced soda or seltzer water; sprigs of borage, balm or verbena may be added if preferred to lemon peel. Nectarines or peaches, cut in slices, or raspberries, may be used. Serve over a block of ice in a large punch bowl.

MOLDED CUCUMBER SALAD

Makes 10-12 servings.

Dissolve 1 package lime gelatin in ¾ cup hot water; let stand until partially set. Combine ¾ cup shredded, unpeeled cucumber with 2 tablespoons grated onion and drain

well. Mix together 1 cup cottage cheese, 1 cup mayonnaise, 1/3 cup slivered almonds, add cucumber and onion, and fold into partially set gelatin. Pour into mold and chill until set. Unmold and garnish with parsley before serving.

CAULIFLOWER MOUSSE

Makes 10-12 servings.

Puree 2½ cups of cooked cauliflower and 2½ cups of cooked potatoes. Use more cauliflower than potato if desired — but never less. Mix together well. Chop together a generous cupful of fresh herbs — chives, parsley, oregano, rosemary, tarragon, etc. and add to the puree. Stir in enough mayonnaise (about 5 tablespoons) to blend the ingredients together. Salt and pepper to taste. Mix well, shape into a loaf on a serving dish, and serve cold garnished with chives and parsley.

SWEET ORANGE JELLY

Makes 10-12 servings.

Soak 1 tablespoonful plus 1 teaspoonful of gelatin in 2/3 cup of cold water. Pour in 2/3 cup of boiling water and stir briskly to dissolve. Then mix in 2 cups of sugar, 6 teaspoonfuls of lemon juice, 2 cups of orange juice, and 4 tablespoonfuls of grated orange peel. You may add rum to taste in place of part of the orange juice. Chill over ice until it starts to jell and then fold in 6 stiffly beaten egg whites. Put it into one or more molds and chill. Turn out on a platter and ring it round with orange sections or with strawberries.

EEL PATTIES

Skin and empty middle-sized eels, cut them into inch lengths, and throw them into salt and water for an hour. Put them into a stew-pan with salt, pepper, mace, a sprig of parsley, and lemon peel; pour over them no more hot water than will cover them. As soon as the bone can be removed (from five to ten minutes) take them out and do so, thus splitting each piece of eel into two. Set them aside, remove the lemon peel &c. from the broth, thicken it with butter and flour, flavor it with lemon juice or a teaspoonful of vinegar, and to this sauce return your eel. Then make pastry in patty-pans, fill with eel and sauce, cover with a top crust and set into a brisk oven. Eel patties are served either hot or cold.

POTATOES SOUFFLÉE

This elegant preparation is not very difficult to execute. Peel potatoes; cut them in the direction of their length, into slices a quarter of an inch thick. Fry them until they are three parts done in moderately hot fat. Take them out, drain, let get nearly cold. Then throw them into very hot fat, and plenty of it; keep them moving till they are well souffléed or swollen, and of a nice light brown, which takes place almost immediately. Take them out, dust them with a little very fine salt, and serve at once.

LOBSTER SALAD

We almost hesitate to give a recipe for this, because everybody thinks he knows how to make it best; and indeed, with good materials, it is not easy to go far wrong. Not a bad plan is this: Pick the shells clean; arrange them, empty, handsomely, on a dish and garnish them with parsley, nasturtium flowers, &c. Put the contents of the shells, properly divided and mixed, into the bottom of a salad bowl; pour over them a liberal quantity of not too piquant sauce, or approved salad mixture. Then hide them under a coverlid of choicest salad hearts, picked leaf by leaf, and augmented with whatever suits your taste. . . . Announce the lobster salad as the bouquet of the feast; everyone will keep a corner for it. When its turn comes, the salad bowl and the dish of shells are placed on the table, you indignantly exclaim, "What a pity! What a shame! What an irremedial misfortune! The cats have eaten the lobster, and left us the shells! I could eat the cats, if caught, out of very spite. As it is, we must eat the salad and smell the shells, as canny folks do with their bread and cheese. Brown, will you have the goodness to mix the salad? I haven't the heart to do it!" Whereupon, to the general comfort, Brown discovers that the lobster salad is nearly as good as if he had compounded it himself.

SALADS

A good salad is a very nice thing; a poor salad is a very bad thing; in any question of the table, the difference is enormous, and ought not to be allowed to exist, especially when the removal of the defect is so easy. A plain cook is apt to think that so simple a thing as a salad may be safely left to take care of itself. . . . In which case the master or mistress of the house, instead of resisting the fool in her folly, had better attend to the salad themselves. In the first place, the vegetable which forms the basis of the salad — whether lettuce, endive, watercress, &c., must be fresh, clean picked, crisp, and at the same time free from all superfluous moisture. A plain cook's intellect will often carry as far as that. Sometimes even, she will provide a few ordinary garnishings, as bits of celery hearts, spring or seedling onions, to chop very fine, slices of cold baked beetroot, nasturtium, borage, or mullein flowers, &c. To relieve a salad from insipidity, sprinkle over it a small quantity of aromatic herb chopped very fine, as tarragon, chervil, balm &c. The golden rule for dressing is to be "prodigal of oil, prudent with salt, avaricious with vinegar." The salad dresser will first measure over the salad four bumping salad-spoonfuls of oil, with pepper

and salt in quantity he knows to be approved. He then mixes the salad with a spoon and fork until every particle of it has come in contact with the oil. One spoonful of good vinegar (in which a little mustard has been mixed) will suffice, toss and mix again. Salad too strongly acidulated may be set down, like Beau Brummell's wisped cravat, as "one of our failures."

Parlor Games and Forfeits

In keeping with our Victorian theme, we planned to follow dinner with traditional parlor games. We did have some reservations about how our guests would react to them. Almost half of the company was under twenty; would they be too sophisticated to want to play? And the adults, would they be bored? We need not have worried. Everyone was in a jovial, tipsy-cake mood and glad to enter into the spirit of the games.

We had decided that the forfeits, or penalties paid for losing at games, were as much fun as the games themselves, so we skipped the games and went directly to the forfeits, sure that they would be an excellent finale for the evening's entertainment. Even Cassell observes that "most of the games appear to be designed for the express purpose of extracting as many forfeits as possible." Before the party we had written on individual slips of paper as many forfeits as there were guests, and hidden the slips in the cornucopias (see page 176) on the Christmas tree. We took the precaution of asking one of our more dignified guests (who, luckily, had a sense of humor) to volunteer as the first player. He drew the ridiculous forfeit, "Play the Learned Pig," and acted out the part with such dramatic flair that he at once had everyone laughing and eager to take a turn.

The following forfeits are only a few of those listed in the *Household Guide;* you need be limited in composing others only by your imagination — and of course caution, lest you cause "The girls to become sad romps or the boys to behave in a boisterous and ungentlemanly manner."

The following are examples of forfeits which may be allotted.

TO CHOOSE ONE OF THREE SIGNS

To do this, he is to stand with his face to the wall, while any lady present makes three signs behind him — of a kiss, of a pinch, and of a box on the ear. He is then asked whether he chooses the first, the second, or the third, not knowing the order in which they have been made, and receives the corresponding action.

TO KISS A LADY THROUGH THE BACK OF A CHAIR

He must wait with his visage inserted in the chair-back, until some lady comes to his rescue; but if the chair be of a fancy pattern, she may dodge him through the framework before giving him his release.

TO SING A SONG OR PLAY A PIECE OF MUSIC

This is given either to elicit the musical capabilities of a lady who is shy, or to make an agreeable interlude in the round of other forfeits. If the lady can really do neither, she is given another forfeit.

TO KISS THE GENTLEMAN YOU LOVE BEST IN THE COMPANY WITHOUT ANYONE KNOWING

There is only one way of paying this penalty, that is to kiss every gentleman in the room, leaving them to settle the question as to "loved best" amongst themselves.

TO PRETEND TO BE A NESTING BIRD

Take a feather, go about the room tickling persons under the chin. When you have elicited five smiles or giggles, you have sufficient "feathers" for your nest and may retire thereto.

PLAY THE LEARNED PIG

The gentleman gets on hands and knees to comport himself as a pig. In response to questions from the company as "Who is the most charming person in the room?" "Who is the prettiest?" the pig responds by grunt-

ing at the person he chooses. When one of the persons he indicates can, or will, give him a shiny dime, he is released from playing a pig.

TO PLAY A KITTEN

You must go about the room mewing and otherwise comporting yourself as a kitten. Each person you approach must pat your head and say "Poor Puss!" The first person who smiles or laughs while doing so releases you from your feline state — but they then must pay a forfeit.

We conclude our list of forfeits with some contrived to include more than one member of the company.

TO FORM A RIFLE CORPS

The lady goes to one end of the room, and calls up a gentleman, who stands opposite her. The gentleman then calls a lady, who stands at his side; and she names a gentleman, who stands opposite her, and so on until all present are included. If there are an uneven number of ladies and gentleman, the more mirth is created by the last persons called standing opposite one of their own sex. When all are called, the word is given by the first gentleman in the rank, "Present arms." All then join hands with the person opposite; and the next command is "Salute," which is done in osculatory fashion.

When several forfeits remain, which it is desired to clear off together, the forfeiters may be called upon to perform a Musical Medley. Each must sing a verse of a song, no two choosing the same melody, but all starting and singing together. The effect is generally so grotesque as to produce shouts of laughter.

We were surprised and amused to find how many of Cassell's forfeits include kissing members of the opposite sex! Not at all the sort of thing we had expected, but then we were also surprised to find how many of the book's recipes had a healthy amount of liquor in them. The Victorians were obviously not as sober and straitlaced as we had been led to believe.

After our guests had romped through the forfeits, they wanted to try another Victorian pastime, so we played Substantives. Young and old alike entered into it with enthusiasm and produced some gems of poetic flight. Not so polished as Cassell's example, perhaps, but flights of fancy nonetheless.

SUBSTANTIVES

An excellent game for an intelligent circle, and one which affords delightful intellectual recreation for persons of ready brains.

A sheet of note paper and two small slips of paper are handed to every player, who is to write on one slip a question and on the other a substantive (noun). The more absurd both the question and substantive can be made, the better the sport. One of the company then collects the questions in one bowl, and the substantives in another. Each player then draws at random one question and one substantive, each must then write a verse in which the question is answered and the substantive introduced. When all are written [you may want to set a time limit to keep the game moving] *, the verses are folded up with the question and substantive inside. They must then be read aloud, first the question, then the substantive, then the verse in which they appear, as in this example:*

The question has been asked, "Will you come into the garden, Maud?" and the substantive suggested is "tadpole." A poet eminent for his observation of Nature, writes:

When the stagnant pool's black face is hid
By its mantle of duck-weed green:
When the sedge and the rush grow thick and lush,
When the frog and the newt are seen;
When none of that musical low-lived race
That dwell in its slime are dumb,
Then Maud, with her cold and clear-cut face,
Will into the garden come,
In its muddy lair a tadpole to snair,
To stock her a-qua-ri-um!

 Here are some of the verses our guests wrote: The question: What is a good girl to do? The substantive: Pension. The poem:

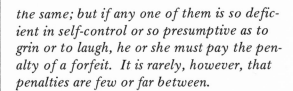
What is a good girl to do?
In London she goes to the loo-
To escape the attentions
Of old men on pensions
Who want to pitch her some woo!

The question: How do you get your money's
worth? The substantive: Cloud.
The poem:

I wake at noon
That's awfully late
The clouds that stay
Make a short day.
Tomorrow, I do intend
To make my day extend.
I'll romp and play-
Be full of mirth
By gosh, I'll get
My money's worth!

The question: Why worry?
The substantive: Corn.
The poem:

ODE ON A GRECIAN CORN

My sandal does not quite fit
Upon my toe, it rubs a bit-
But I must go to Thermopylae
To guard the pass until I die.
     So why worry about a corn
     About to form.
I won't worry-
I'm in a hurry.

For those of you wanting to be truly
authentic, here is a sampling of some of the
more popular Victorian parlor games and the
traditional method of "Crying the Forfeits."

THE COURTIERS

*One of the company is selected to be the
king or queen, and occupies a chair in the center of the room, the rest being seated round
the sides of the apartment. Whatever move-
ment may be made by the monarch must be
imitated by the courtiers; and it is the gist of
the game that this should be done without
anyone losing that assumption of decorous
gravity which becomes the scene. The monarch may yawn, sneeze, blow his nose, or
wipe his eyes, and the courtiers must all do*

*the same; but if any one of them is so defic-
ient in self-control or so presumptive as to
grin or to laugh, he or she must pay the penalty of a forfeit. It is rarely, however, that
penalties are few or far between.*

THE MESSENGER

*The party are seated in line, or round the
sides of the room, and some one previously
appointed enters with the message, "My
master sends me to you, Madam," or "Sir,"
as the case may be, directed to any individual he may select at his option. "What for?"
is the natural inquiry. "To do as I do;" and
with this the messenger commences to perform some antic, which the lady or gentleman
must imitate. The person whose duty it is to
obey, commands his neighbor to the right or
to the left to "Do as I do," also; and so on
until the whole company are in motion, when
the messenger leaves the room, re-entering it
with fresh injunctions. While the messenger
is in the room he must see his master's will
obeyed, and no one may stop from the move-
ment without suffering a forfeit.*

SPEAKING BUFF

*At this game, the eyes of one of the play-
ers are bandaged, as in "blind man," and he is
seated in the center of the room, the party
then taking their places. "Buff" holds a wand
or a stick in one hand, and when all are seated, he points with this to one side of the room,
or touches one of the players, at the same
time uttering three words according to his
fancy. The person towards whom he points
must then repeat these words; and if "Buff"
can discover his or her identity by the tones
of the voice, he is released from his position,
and the person detected takes his place.*

TWIRLING THE TRENCHER

*This is a brisk game, requiring activity
without ingenuity. A circle is formed in the
room, and a good space is left clear in the
midst. A trencher or round wooden plater
is obtained. When all the party is seated, one
of the company stands up in the center and
twirls the tray round upon the floor, at the*

same time calling out the name of any other person present, who must rise and pick up the trencher before it falls to the ground, otherwise he or she pays a forfeit. The person who twirls the trencher returns to his seat and the one who picks it up has the privilege of making a call.

FORFEITS

It will have been observed that some of the games already described lead up to the payment of forfeits. . . . "Crying the Forfeits," as it is called, often forms the most amusing part of an evening's entertainment, and is, therefore, usually reserved until the last. It is conducted in the following manner:

Each player who has to pay a forfeit deposits some small article, or trinket, in the hands of one of the company appointed as collector — say a handkerchief, a knife, a pencilcase, or any article which can be readily identified. One article is to be given for every forfeit incurred, and it is redeemed when the particular task assigned to the owner has been duly performed. . . . When an average of one to each member of the party has been reached, if the number is between a dozen and twenty, it is time to stop the collection.

Two persons, chosen from the rest of the company for their knowledge of suitable and amusing forfeits, and generally ladies, cry the forfeits thus: One is seated, and the various articles collected are placed in her lap. The other is blindfolded, and kneels down before her companion. . . .

The person seated takes one of the articles from the collection before her, and, holding it up so that the company may recognise the owner, usually cries, "Here is a thing, and a very pretty thing; what shall be done by the owner of this very pretty thing?" This established form of words, which dates further back than the memory of man, may, however, be reduced to the latter clause alone, if that plan is preferred. The blindfolded lady asks, "Is it fine or superfine?" or "Is it a lady's or a gentleman's?" for this much she is allowed to know, that she may name a suitable forfeit. Having received an answer, she declares the task which the owner must perform. The spirit in which the forfeit game should be conducted is to extract as much harmless fun from them as possible, avoiding everything rough and unseemly, or in which a mind exceptionally sensitive can find a cause of offense.

Temporary Decorations for an Impromptu Ballroom

How many gymnasiums have you helped transform into temporary ballrooms? We couldn't begin to count the decorating committees we've worked on for school and social events — usually on a limited budget. It seems that the Victorians struggled with the same problem. Cassell's version of the gym-to-ballroom transformation is somewhat grandiose. Indeed, even he, after blithely asserting that the changes will takes "just a few hours" (putting us forcibly in mind of the coordinators of some the committees on which we've worked), runs down at the end of his presentation and acknowledges that time, patience, and many willing hands are needed. Even so, some of these ideas are well worth borrowing for your next decorating project, and if you are ambitious enough to carry out Cassell's entire plan, you will really astonish your guests!

It frequently happens in families where festivities are rather the exception than the rule, that it is necessary to convert a school room, a hall, or sometimes even a barn to do service as a ball room, a concert room, or a place for private theatricals. We propose showing how such a room may be tastefully decorated at an insignificant cost, in such a manner as we have proved by experience to be at the same time practicable and effective.

Let us suppose that it is desired to decorate a large room presenting nothing beyond four bare whitewashed walls. We shall show how in a few hours, the lower portion of the sides of this room may be made to appear as though hung with crimson drapery, and the upper to be painted with an effective diaper; how the walls may in appearance be divided into compartments by marble pilasters; and how a temporary fountain may be erected

at one end, rising above a bank of flowers and evergreens.

In order to effect these decorations, the first thing to be done will be to divide the walls into upper and lower portions; the latter should be about six feet high, more or less, according to the dimensions of the room. The upper portion we first propose to decorate by means of stenciling.

An effective pattern for stenciling is that shown in our illustration of a portion of wall when decorated (Fig. 1), or in more detail in Figs. 2 and 3; it consists of a heraldic lion and a flower. Stencil plates may be made of cardboard. The stencil plate is made by cutting away those portions which are to be represented by color on the walls, and which are shown light in our woodcuts; small portions are left at the juncture of detached parts, as the legs of the lion, for the purpose of holding the plate together. The patterns can be enlarged to scale and then cut out. The stenciling is done by merely holding or fixing the plate with tacks against the wall and dashing on the color with a good sized brush. It is well before commencing to stencil to measure and mark out upon the walls the places where the central points of the figures in the pattern should fall. It is better to commence the operation against the ceiling, and to work downwards, to avoid splashes or injury to the work as it proceeds.

The upper portion of the walls being thus stenciled, the next proceeding will be to cover the lower portion with imitation drapery. Nothing will look better for this than a common wall paper, which has a simple pattern in two shades of crimson. This is to be pasted against the wall, and when dry the effect of drapery may be given to it with black paint and a small brush marking bold and distinct lines upon the paper, as shown

in Fig. 1. The illusion will be completed by pasting a bordering along its top; one of crimson and yellow with gold studs at intervals, would look well; and a second border of yellow paper along its base, which may be picked out with a few strokes of the brush and black paint to give the appearance of fringe.

We will next divide the walls into bays or compartments by pilasters. This we can do with pieces of lumber about 6" wide by 2½" thick, and as tall as required. These are to be covered by tacking marbled paper over them; or their fronts may be covered with paper on which an ornamental pilaster has been printed, like that given in Fig. 1. They are then to be placed against the wall at stated intervals, and each may be fixed with two strong nails at top and bottom. A wreath of evergreens fastened round the top on one of these pilasters makes a pretty capital, and conceals its junction with the ceiling, while long tendrils of ivy tied together, falling down at each side, and held fast by a tack or two, will conceal any imperfection in its juncture with the wall. Pedestals may be made of whitewashed boxes or beer barrels wreathed with evergreen. A kind of ornamental cornice, composed of mottoes, neatly cut out of colored paper may be made to run from pilaster to pilaster, just beneath the ceiling, and two festoons of evergreens between each pair of pilasters, looped to a nail in the center, from which a basket of flowers would have a very pretty appearance.

Few decorative objects are more pleasing and refreshing in a hot and brilliantly lighted room than a fountain. A temporary fountain, though its erection may at first sight appear to involve much trouble and expense, is really a simple affair.

Although the original instructions were very ingenious, they also were very complex, not at all a "simple affair." Besides, they were wasteful of water. Today all we need is an inflatable child's wading pool, and a small recirculating pump. If these are well camouflaged, along the lines suggested below, they make a splendid fountain.

Flowers, or shrubs in pots, must be placed round the fountain in the manner shown in Fig. 4, large ones standing as high as its edges being nearest it, and decreasing gradually in size. Sawdust must be spread over and between the pots, so as to fill up the interstices, and when a covering of green moss has been placed over the sawdust, hiding the edges of the tub, the whole will have the effect of a green mossy bank from which plants are springing, sloping up to the margin of a pretty, natural looking fountain, which will be rendered complete by placing in it some gold fish.

Pretty effects may be produced by the use of paper lanterns. These may be made of any shape, by first forming a framework of wire, and pasting tissue-paper of various colors over the skeleton, as fancy may dictate. [See Fig. 6.] Large square or octagonal lanterns, Figs. 5 & 7, are made by forming the bottom of a piece of board with upright pieces at the corners to support the sides. First paste stout brown paper, perforated as shown in Fig. 5, on the wooden frame, and then covering the perforations on the inside with colored tissue-paper.

The artist has indicated a landscape at the end of the room behind the fountain [see Fig. 8]. *Obviously it is not intended that a valuable work of art should be placed in such a position; but if there is a sufficient amount of amateur talent to supply a spirited sketch, with landscape and figures, it might be well employed in this direction.*

Some patience, ingenuity, and time will of course be required for these decorations, but these are generally forthcoming in abundance on occasions when such labor is required; and the effect of a room when so decorated, though it might not pass muster by daylight, or when closely examined, would be sure to be successful when seen once only and by artificial light, and when it would have for the spectators the charm of novelty and surprise by being met with in an apartment where no ornamental features were known to have previously existed.

FIG. 2

FIG. 3

FIG. 1

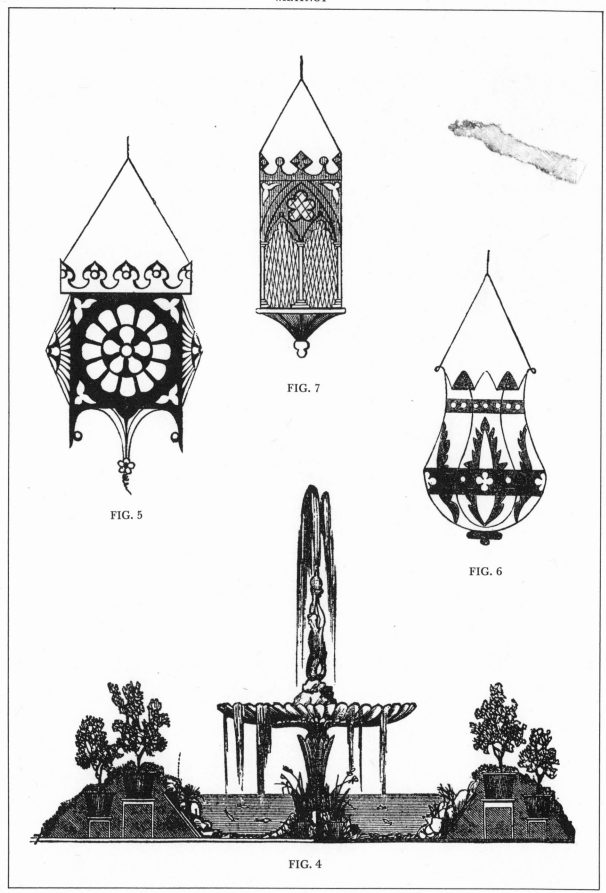

FIG. 7

FIG. 5

FIG. 6

FIG. 4

FIG. 8

Principles of Good Taste in Household Furnishings

Victorian furniture is certainly not to everyone's taste. But just in case your great aunt has left you a sizable bequest on the condition you use the furniture that *she* had inherited, here are a few of the 1870s views on interior design. This period has been much maligned for want of taste and discipline in design — unfairly! There were very definite principles, but, unfortunately, not every one followed them. We may not agree with the writer's view of suitability and simplicity, but he certainly had one, and if you want to recreate a Victorian setting, what better authority could you find?

Let us assume that our walls are covered with papers of tasteful designs, and that carpets have been chosen of unobtrusive designs, which are adapted for horizontal surfaces, and for being trodden upon. We have now to introduce our furniture, and in doing so keep in view the color and character of our background. The wall and carpet should contrast with the furniture and serve to relieve it; but, in the objects themselves, there should, in each room, be a degree of uniformity of design. If there is too much diversity, the room will look as if it had been furnished piecemeal, and without due regard to the unity and completeness of the whole. Nothing destroys the unity so much as to introduce two or three kinds of wood. There should also be uniformity in the character of the forms, and also in the enrichments. Should the table be rectangular. . . it would be more in keeping if the leading lines of the chairs, sideboard, &c., be straight; and whatever the kind or style of enrichment employed on the one, it should be adopted on all.

To obtain this uniformity of style, the two chief things to be attended to are: firstly, that the enrichments be equally simple or florid, secondly, that the ornament itself be of one style or character. Great want of taste is often manifested by the indiscriminate mixture of various styles of ornament between which there is not the least affinity. A comparison of Fig. 4 and 5 will strikingly illustrate the incongruity which may arise form the violation of this rule. In these examples, we see two treatments so utterly opposed in spirit that to place them in the same room would show the greatest ignorance of ornament, and lack of judgement.

Let us illustrate our meaning. Suppose that our taste inclines us to admire ornament which consists chiefly of natural forms. . . like the Gothic artists of the decorated period, who introduced flowers, foliage, animals, and the human form, in every conceivable combination. Adopting this naturalism as our leading principle, we introduce natural forms throughout the enrichments. We choose for wallpaper a pattern of some simple diaper, consisting of a geometric basis filled in with leaves. For our carpet we choose a pattern in which flowers and foliage are also arranged on a geometric basis. We choose for our table one with animals crouching underneath (as in Fig. 1), or, if less elaborate, say with animals' feet only (as in Fig. 2); and our chairs have similar terminals to their legs, and a little carved foliage or fruit on the legs and back (as in Fig. 3); and the sofa or couch is designed in the same spirit. . . . Fantastic shapes should be studiously avoided; and as simplicity rarely offends, it is far better, as a rule, to select forms which are simple and unassuming.

Some seem to think that you cannot have too much of a good thing, and that the more ornament you can introduce the better. This, however, is a great mistake, for such excess of elaboration marks the degeneracy of most styles of ornament, while

in the best periods of art simplicity has generally been one of the leading principles.

The sideboard in Fig. 5 is an example of
this excessive elaboration, and looks as if it
had been made and then smothered with ornament. So far as it is possible, it is best to let
the ornament arise out of the construction
(as in Figs. 1, 2, 3, 4, and 6.) and not to appear as if stuck upon the surface (as in Fig. 5)

without any other connection with the subject. Instead of the moulding of the back itself being enriched, whatever beauty it might
have had has been disfigured by flowers and
foliage being stuck all over it. . . .

Again, we must be careful that ornamental forms in relief — such as carved work
— do not project so much as to be liable to
injure the dresses of those who pass near them.

FIG. 1

FIG. 2

FIG. 3

FIG. 4

FIG. 6

FIG. 5

The General Servant

You may come to wonder, as we did, how the ladies of the period found the hours to pursue so many time-consuming crafts. One reason was that all but the most modest households were blessed with at least one servant. And being a servant was no small job. We were awed by the lengthy list of tasks to be performed by this poor soul, who, as you will see, had little time for "fancy work." A farm girl, gone into service in the city, was considered lucky and was thought to have taken a step upward in the social scale, but it is hard to believe she was happier in service than she was at home. Cassell says:

Formerly country girls were content to live from one year's end to another in the same situation from sheer inability to defray the expenses of travelling any distance. Now-a-days, railway trains have thrown the servant market open, and, consequently, even remote provinces are drained of household help. The rush is to the large towns, and especially to London, where wages are high, and dress and pleasures plentiful and cheap.

What good the clothes or cheap pleasures were to her is hard to conceive when one reads the Victorian concept of the amount of free time a servant should have.

A mistress should be careful not to bind herself to spare her servant on a certain day in every month, as is sometimes demanded. "Once a month when convenient" is a better understanding. Most servants, in addition to the monthly holiday, ask to be allowed to go to church of a Sunday once in the day. This request is reasonable; and if a servant really goes to a place of worship, some inconvenience should be borne by her employer to secure her this liberty. The absence ought not to extend beyond the time occupied in the church service.

And here is Cassell's list of what could fairly be expected of a servant.

The duties of a general servant being numerous, it is desirable that a well considered plan embodying the principal work of the house should be provided. The rules of the house and order of work should be legibly and tersely written on cardboard, suspended on the kitchen wall.

Six o'clock is the latest hour at which the servant should arise. By getting her work ready in the evening, she is enabled to set about it at once in the morning. She should put every thing in its place at night, wash up plates and dishes, hang up jugs, and tidy her kitchen. If, after having raked out the fire, she lays it with fresh coals, a great point will be gained. All except the front bars of the range can be polished whilst the fire is drawing up. Twice a week the range, boiler, and oven should be thoroughly cleaned, and the soot from the mouth of the chimney be cleared away with a sweep's brush, as far as the arm can reach.

Whilst the fire is drawing up, the servant should remain near to give it a timely stir be-

fore setting the kettle on, employing her time in the meanwhile in cleaning boots, knives, or any other occupation of the kind.

She should next wash her hands and open the curtains of the breakfast room. She should then take a large sweeping cloth, and cover up any ornaments or furniture likely to be spoilt by dust. The hearth rug should be folded up and laid aside to be shaken. A coarse cloth should then be laid in its place, on which the black-lead box, the cinder sifter, and fire-irons should rest whilst in use. To clean a parlor grate, fire-irons, and fender thoroughly, will take about twenty minutes.

Sweeping the carpet is the next proceeding. A good manager will never commence this work without having a plentiful supply of tea-leaves to strew on the floor. These collect the dust which would otherwise settle on the hangings.

Having proceeded so far in the breakfast-room, the hall and entrance claim attention. Even if there not be time to whiten the door-steps before breakfast, sweeping should be done and the mats and rugs shaken outside. . . .

The dirty work of the morning now being at an end, the servant should change to a cleaner gown, apron and cap, and dust the breakfast-room. She is now ready to lay the cloth, bring in breakfast, and do her upstairs work generally. If there be sufficient time, this is the best opportunity she will have for her own breakfast. Servants cannot be healthy if they snatch their food whilst running about.

Directly breakfast is finished and cleared away, she must open the windows of the bedrooms and strip all the beds. . . . The feather beds should be well shaken and turned. The chamber crockery must be emptied and cleaned with hot water and soda. The water bottles and tumblers should be emptied and cleaned. . . . In most families where there are daughters, the general servant gets help in making the beds.

If no special cleaning is to be done, the bedrooms should be dusted and put in order, the servant collecting lamps, candlesticks, and other articles that have to be cleaned in the kitchen. When the upstairs work is so far done, she should begin a general washing up in the kitchen. The mistress or daughters will probably in the meanwhile dust the ornaments in the drawing room, and aid in giving an air of order and refinement to the room.

The hour at which the family dines determines whether the servant shall do the principal house cleaning in the morning or afternoon. Some forethought is required to set a servant free to do special cleaning without neglecting the dinner. If a general servant is required to wait at table, it is unreasonable to expect that she can be very tidy at midday. But if the dinner hour is late, she may be able to dress herself before dishing up, having previously cleared her kitchen. No washing up beyond china and glass should be expected afterwards. The dishes should be stacked until morning when time for washing them and the sauce-pans &c. should be allowed. Under these circumstances the servant can wait upon the family in the evening, and employ the rest of her time in repairing or making her clothes.

Active Recreations for Ladies

Cassell's *Household Guide* contains several especially revealing pieces on active recreations for ladies, which give a good picture of the athletic prowess of Victorian women — and of their sportswear! How on earth did anyone do *anything* with all those clothes on? Cassell writes:

Helplessness and inactivity are no longer looked upon as feminine virtues. Exercise is now recognized to be as important in a woman's education as in a man's, many bodily defects and much of her weak health is attributable to the want of it.

He emphasizes that exercise is a good thing in moderation — that it should not be overly strenuous — and then, in a piece called "Riding for Ladies," gives instructions on

hunting and "leaping." Now, if there is any activity much more strenuous than spending half a day galloping about the countryside, leaping stone walls and ditches, we're not sure what it might be. Perhaps no one gave this apparent contradiction a second thought, since risking one's neck in the hunting field had long been considered perfectly proper for ladies who could afford it. Riding, in any case, had other advantages.

Riding

There are few exercises which are more delightful or more health-giving, and none in which Englishwomen more particularly ex-

cel; further, ladies rarely show to such advantage as when mounted.

Here are some of the other activities recommended for the fairer sex.

Calisthenics

The word is derived from the Greek "kalos," beautiful; and "sthenos," strength; the object of these exercises being to secure physical beauty by developing the limbs and muscles of the human frame, giving strength and power, and ensuring a graceful carriage, erect bearing, and freedom to the figure. Such exercise cures many deformities of mind and person. . . .

Calisthenics, irregularly conducted, will do more harm than good. The constitution must be coaxed, not strained, and we present an orderly system of exercises to be followed.

A tasteful ensemble for excuting calisthenics.

Archery

This graceful and elegant art, which, when no longer used for warlike purposes, became a fashionable and a royal game, deserves more attention by private families. It would be as easy to set up a target on a lawn as to cover it with croquet bridges, and an archery meeting, on however small a scale, with or

without its pretty green tunic, hat and feathers has an unspeakable charm.

The dress worn at archery meetings is very pretty and becoming — a green cloth jacket, with a black velvet dress, and a green hat and black feather. In warm weather the jacket is silk, worn over a white muslin dress.

Sea Bathing

This is a wholesome recreation for ladies, if not overdone. Fortunately, great reforms have been made within the last few years in ladies bathing dresses. Great reform was needed, if utility, health, and comfort were to be preserved. The long loose gown formerly worn was apt to cling to the wearer as she left the water and cause a chill, and swimming in such a garment was almost impossible. The very greatest objection of all was, that occasionally the air filled or the wind caught it, as the bather rose above the surface of the waves, and bore it up above the crest of the water like a balloon.

The French fashion, now in vogue, is pretty and modest and consists of a pair of

trousers, cut from any pattern that fits like boys' knickerbockers cut long, and a blouse, cut like a boys' tunic, and long enough to reach the knees, and belted at the waist.

Some bathing dresses are plain, some piquant. There is no reason why they should not be prettily ornamented. Ladies of taste will not desire to call any particular attention to themselves in the water by conspicuous dress, although they may properly desire not to look unsightly objects to their companions, nor to any other who may see them. Nothing is more suitable than dark blue serge. This may be trimmed with scarlet military braid without being remarkably conspicuous.

Long hair may be left floating, tied back by a ribbon, as it looks prettiest, but is inconvenient. Or it may be twisted into a coil on the crown of the head; or it may be placed in an oilskin cap, edged with scarlet.

Coverings for the feet of bathers are essential at most watering places. A loose boot, of colored felted flannel, of a medieval cut, is easily slipped on or off, and is very inexpensive.

Bagatelle

This is a very interesting indoor activity, and when well played a great deal of science may be displayed. Bagatelle serves as an introduction to billiards, and is good practice for players of that more scientific game.

To use the cue, stand firmly at the end
of the table in an easy, graceful attitude, with
the left foot a little advanced, and the head
slightly inclined forward; but do not stoop.
The illustration also shows the position of the
left hand.

Croquet

No game ever worked its way sooner into general acceptance than croquet. Although
of comparatively recent introduction into England, there was scarcely a lawn where the
game was not played, while at watering places
and other public localities provision was made
for strangers to enjoy the pleasures of the
game in association with each other. And this
great popularity was not to be attributed to
novelty alone. The game at that time stood by
itself, as one in which people of both sexes
could participate in an out-of-door pastime
and find both exercise and amusement, while
ample scope was given for the display of individual skill and ingenuity.

Ice Skating

The ladies, formerly so seldom seen upon
the ice, have of late years made an immense
advance in courage and perseverance. A good
lady skater is no longer an extraordinary
sight.

41

PART TWO

HOUSEHOLD DECORATIVE ARTS

A collection of over forty Victorian crafts including:

Decorative Shellwork

Potichomanie

Point Lace Paper Fly Cages

D'oyleys from Natural Foliage

A Water Bouquet

Souvenirs and Tasteful Trifles

Fish-Scale Embroidery

and others.

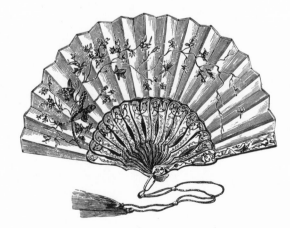

Introduction

WHAT A WEALTH of unusual decorative crafts the *Household Guide* contained! The projects were of a highly intriguing variety and quality—sometimes serious, sometimes frivolous—and we have tried to include the best of them.

All of the crafts might be re-created using the original instructions, but these were often so lengthy and confusing that today's unwary reader can become hopelessly tangled in the convoluted verbiage.

What we have done is modernize and simplify the directions, using newer methods and materials wherever necessary, while retaining as much as possible of Cassell's appropriate, often amusing, text and his marvelous illustrations.

We have written directions for some of the projects, some projects have a combination of old and new directions, and others are given with the original text and only an occasional suggestion from us. We have changed things wherever we felt it would be of help to the reader, without, we hope, losing the essential Victorian flavor.

We have included a few projects without having done them because they are interesting or amusing and because someone else might want to try them (see Fish-Scale Embroidery, Aeolian Harps, Grottoes, and Summer Houses). We have tried to make our instructions as clear as possible. There may be other ways to do these projects but here are the techniques that worked for us, and we pass them on to you.

The supplies needed for these projects are, for the most part, easily obtainable — things that can be found at the hardware store, the craft shop, the artist's supply store or the junk shop. We have suggested possible sources for any items that are unusual or hard to find.

We did have one recurring experience doing the projects in this book; the difference between success and utter frustration often lay in the tools we used. The items on the following list are not all strictly necessary, but what a joy to have them! We are convinced that they save their price many times over in wasted materials and time.

All of these first items are available at stores specializing in drafting supplies and in many art supply stores.

An accurate ruler with a metal edge and cork backing. $1.00.
Technical drafting pencil. $1.00 to $3.00.
Assorted leads and sandpaper sharpener for drafting pencil. $2.00.
Technical fountain pen with No. 2 point. $9.00 to $12.00. This may seem like an expensive item, but anyone who has struggled with an old-fashioned drafting pen will know that the new ones are worth every penny.
Drawing board — 20" by 26" is a useful size. About $10.00
T square — 26" long. About $8.00 to $10.00. If you get a larger board, get a longer T square.
Triangle — 30 by 60 by 90 degree. $1.00 to $2.00.
Different size points are available at about $4.50 each.
Special ink for the fountain pen. $1.00.
Lettering pens and a crow quill pen. These can be purchased either in sets with a pen handle and six or seven nibs or separately. $2.00 to $3.00.
Waterproof India ink. $1.00.
Craftsman's knife with a variety of blades. X-Acto puts out a set with two handles and twelve blades. $3.50.

These next items are readily available at any hardware store. The prices we quote are for good quality tools, neither the cheapest available nor the most costly.

Utility razor knife with a large grip handle and extra blades. $1.50.
Needle-nose pliers with wirecutter. $6.00.
Steel yardstick or square. $4.00 to $8.00.
Good quality paintbrushes — ¾" and 1½" wide. $3.00 to $5.00 each.
Several cheap paintbrushes — ½" to 2" wide, for applying glue, etching compound, etc. $.50 to $.90 each.

We wish we had a penny for every time someone said to us: "But *you're* artists; I can't draw a straight line." We answered: "Nonsense!"

The first fallacy in the thinking of the anxious is that craft projects, no matter how intricate or elaborate, are works of creative genius. That's simply not so. What craft projects require is usually no more than careful attention to detail and a modicum of imagination.

Which brings us to the next obstacle. We have all been brought up to believe that to copy is bad. Again, nonsense! All the great design motifs that have been used through the centuries have been copied a

million times by a million artists, and we defy anyone, short of a creative genius, to devise something totally new.

So now we are faced with our only real problem: how to copy successfully. Some people can sit down and reproduce a shape by simply looking at it and moving a pencil in the right directions. Others have not trained themselves to do this, and for the latter there are several alternative methods of arriving at the same end.

The simplest and most direct method, and one that we often employ, is tracing directly from another picture. The design for our Black and Gilded Box (see page 99) was executed in this way. First you trace a pattern, then you transfer it to the surface to be decorated. Commercial carbon paper is seldom suitable for this operation, as the color is very strong and is likely to bleed through any paint applied subsequently. You can easily make your own carbon paper that will produce a light, erasable line. Scribble with a soft lead pencil all over a sheet of tracing paper. Don't worry about the pencilings being even. When the paper is covered, saturate a paper towel or small rag with paint thinner or lighter fluid and use the saturated material to smear the penciling around until it's fairly even. Don't wipe it all off of course. Let the paper dry and, voila, homemade no-mess carbon paper.

If, as it often happens, you want a design from another source made larger or smaller, there are two possible solutions. First, you can take the original picture to a printer who can, for a few dollars, either blow-up or reduce it to your specifications. We had this done for the corner and border motifs of our Illuminated Backgammon Board (see page 106).

The second way of changing size is useful for more drastic enlargements or reductions, and is strictly do-it-yourself! In this method, on a piece of tracing paper you draw a grid of measured squares to lay over the drawing you want to reproduce. Make a second grid of the same number of squares but with the size of the squares enlarged or reduced according to your desire. Then reproduce the lines of the drawing, square by square, on the changed grid. For example, if you have a design motif that measures 3" by 5" and you want to enlarge it to fit a 9" by 15" box: draw a grid of ½" squares on tracing paper and fix it over the drawing. On a larger piece of paper, draw a grid of as many 1½" squares as you have ½" squares. Then, simply by making the lines cross the corresponding squares in the same manner as they do on the original, you can achieve a very accurate enlargement.

If you still can't bring yourself to take pencil in hand, there is yet another alternative that will help you with many of the projects in this book: découpage. For this you simply cut out decorative motifs from pictures or magazines, glue them on, and seal them using either a commercial découpage finish, or some type of varnish. Our Chinese Album (see page 90) provides detailed instructions for this technique.

The real joy and reward of making things for yourself comes at that sublime moment when a connoisseur-of-antiques friend asks, "Where did you find that perfectly divine Victorian box?" You don't have to tell that you made it yourself— but it's hard to resist.

Imitation Ebony and Ivory Chessboard

The Victorian love of embellishments included an odd fondness for *imitations* of the exotic, a predilection that perhaps is explained by the fact that rare and beautiful inlaid woods and fine Oriental porcelains were beyond the means of all but the wealthy. Whatever the reason, Cassell contained many articles on how to imitate such originals.

An imitation of ebony and ivory inlay. . . is easily accomplished by anyone with a moderate amount of taste. Patient care is the chief requirement, and the result is highly ornamental. This mode of decoration may be applied to a great variety of useful purposes, and many articles of the simplest and cheapest kind may be made to assume a very ornamental appearance by its aid. Leaves and grasses may be selected from the garden, and when flattened out and arranged, be made to supply a large number of highly interesting decorative designs. Fig. 1 is a design of this kind. The edges of deal [pine] bookshelves look very pretty when decorated in this way, and a pattern of this kind may be made by first tracing a waved line, and placing on this line, apparently springing from it, tracings from a series of small leaves flattened out for this purpose. Such borders may be adopted from other decorative work.

Chessboard

Cassell himself suggested enlarging his charming design for a chessboard, but we felt that it would be more interesting to make up our own with leaves we had gathered. Doing it this way gives a much more personalized result and you will always be able to view your own design with fond memories.

You will need:

Fir plywood, grade A; 24" square of ½"
Fine waterproof sandpaper
White primer, sealer
Pressed leaves
Black India ink
Matte découpage finish (Modge Podge)
Felt, 24" square
Decorative molding eight feet of ½" wide quarter round
Small finishing nails
Crow-quill drawing pen
Draftsman's ruling pen or technical fountain pen
Watercolor brushes, sizes No. 0 and No. 2
Clear acrylic spray finish

Pre-cut squares of plywood are sometimes available at lumberyards. Lumberyards will also cut a scrap piece to size for you at a nominal charge. In any case, be sure that the face of the wood is grade A and has no deep scratches or nicks. If you are lucky, you may discover birch or ash plywood, but these woods will cost more and are harder to find.

Sand the board lightly, to smooth the surfaces and edges. Wipe free of all dust. Be sure to sand with the grain of the wood. Paint the face of the board with white primer sealer. Wipe off the excess with a clean cloth, again working with the grain. This stain lightens the plywood and seals it so that the ink won't blur.

When it is dry again sand it lightly. Lay out the chessboard square using a T square and triangle. The overall measurement of the completed board is 24" square; the chessboard in the center is 12" square. Each black square is 1¼" wide. This leaves a 6" border all around for the leaf design.

Next go for a walk through your garden or the countryside; even if you have only a window box or house plants you may be able to collect a variety of specimens. Gather all the leaves, even roadside weeds and grasses, that you feel would make attractive motifs. You will need at least thirty-two different small, perfect leaves, 1" or less, to fit in the small squares, and larger leaves and sprays for the border. The greater the variety, the more interesting the design will be.

A 24" square chessboard decorated by using the imitation of ebony and ivory technique with a design of traced leaves.

(You could do a design with nothing but herbs for a gourmet friend.)

Press the leaves between layers of newspaper and weigh with stacks of books or magazines. The pressing can be done overnight — you don't need dry leaves, just flat ones to make them easy to trace around.

Using the pressed leaves, lay out your design on the board; shift them around and try various combinations of sizes and shapes. You may want to experiment on paper first. When you have decided on the design, trace each leaf outline lightly in pencil. Go over the outline with India ink and a fine drawing pen. Outline each square with India ink; a draftsman's ruling pen or a technical fountain pen is most helpful for this. Fill in the background with a fine watercolor brush. Give the background a second coat of ink to in-

tensify the color. Draw in the leaf veins free-hand, using either a pen or a very fine brush.

Nail and glue the molding around the edges of the board, mitering the corners. Give the molding two coats of ink.

Give the board at least ten coats of matte découpage finish, letting it dry clear between coats. When the last coat is dry, wet the surface with water squeezed from a sponge and sand the board carefully and thoroughly. The surface will cloud and become very slippery and smooth. Wipe off the residue with a clean sponge and allow it to dry. Seal the board with a coat of clear acrylic spray finish.

The final step is to glue a square of felt to the back of the board.

You could make the board into an attractive occasional table just by the addition of ready-made legs.

FIG. 1

FIG. 3

IMITATION EBONY AND IVORY

FIG. 2

Decorative Shellwork

Victorian ladies seemed to have labored under the delusion that if one shell was beautiful, lots of shells were more so and a whole Parthenon of shells, the most!

Several classes of choice ornaments may be manufactured of shells. Success in this work mainly depends on taste in the arrangement. For different purposes the arrangement will necessarily vary; but, as a general rule, it is advisable to assort the shells into the several species and colors. . . . As with flowers, those of pale lavender color are invaluable in contrasting with deep-colored flowers and leaves; so with shells, the glittering, silvery, pale lavender colored ones of opal hue, have an equally superior value. The sides of boxes and all plain surfaces may be well adorned with oval, oblong, or other figures, moulded or bordered with shells of suitable size and appropriate color. . . .

There are some shells which form elegant feet for boxes or tea-caddies. Boxes and pincushions are the usual articles into which shells are manufactured, but they are well suited to many other purposes.

Shell Box

We recommend doing a small piece for your first shell project. You will be surprised to discover how many shells it will take. The shells that you have found on the beach are the most interesting, of course, but unless you are a very industrious collector, the chances are you will have only a few of each kind and those of greatly varying size. For an effective design, we have found that the piece must be outlined and filled in with a great many small shells of uniform size and color. Shells can be bought packaged this way in some craft stores. Another good source is inexpensive shell necklaces, usually from Hawaii or the

Philippines. Although the Victorian shellwork was often painted or dyed, in this instance we preferred to leave the shells in natural colors and restricted ourselves to white, gray, brown, and mauve shells.

You will need:

Shells — It is almost impossible to estimate the number of shells that you will need as it depends so much on the types available. We used approximately two-hundred ¼" shells for the top and as many small olive shells for borders and fillers on the sides. We used about 18 matched pairs of varying sizes of larger shells and 5 single specimens for the top and each side. We needed about 100 little brown auger shells to border the bottom.

Cardboard, about 8" by 18" and 1/8" in thickness.
Lightweight cardboard, about 10" square.
Fancy paper or fabric for lining, 20" wide by 8"long.
Cotton fabric for a hinge, 3" by 4".
Masking tape, 1" wide.
Razor knife
White glue
Brush
Light-beige enamel, flat or semi-gloss, ½ pint.
Tweezers
Tracing paper
Foam rubber

Trace the patterns in Fig. 1 (page 57) for the top, bottom, and sides of the box and transfer them on to the 1/8" cardboard with carbon paper. You will need two of each shape with the exception of the bottom, which requires only one. Cut the pieces out carefully with a sharp razor knife making sure that the edges are clean and the corners perfectly square. Save the paper patterns as you will need them later.

Join the front, back, and sides with masking tape, both inside and out, running the tape from top to bottom the length of the joint. The front and back pieces overlap the sides as shown in Fig. 2.

A small shellwork box in the Victorian manner using
common shells in natural colors of white, gray, brown,
and mauve.

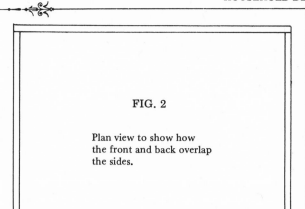

FIG. 2

Plan view to show how
the front and back overlap
the sides.

On ours we used one 2" long tulip shell and several small augers. Now fill in the space between the border and the center motif with shells of another color. We did our box with gray limpets, going in size from 3/8" on the outside to 1/2" toward the center.

Plan the front, back, and sides in the same manner. Here again, the design works best if the piece is outlined in a single color and size shell. We used 3/8" white olives around a center of gray limpets, mauve mussels, and white clams. The cutout base is fringed with brown auger shells. The box will be more effective if all the small border and filler shells face in the same direction and are placed very close together.

Now start to glue the shells in place, working on the back of the box first. Lay the box on its face and brush a fairly heavy layer of white glue, just wide enough to accomodate the top row of shells along the rim of the box and lay the shells in as close together as you can. You may need to handle these small shells with tweezers, and keep a wet towel handy to wipe your fingers free of glue. This top row of shells must be quite flat or they will prevent the lid of the box from opening. When the back is completed,

Fit the bottom piece in at the level indicated on patterns A and B by the broken bottom lines. Tape the bottom securely in place with masking tape both inside and out.

Run a line of tape around the top edge to seal the cut edge of cardboard, cut at each corner and stick it neatly down on both the inside and outside as shown in Fig. 3.

Tape the two lid pieces together, one on top of the other. This double thickness makes the lid a great deal more substantial and improves its appearance. Run tape neatly all around the edges, clipping at the corners so that it lies flat.

Glue the 3" by 4" strip of cotton fabric the length of the top back edge of the box, leaving half its width above the rim. Then glue the remainder of the fabric to the inside of the lid, forming a fabric hinge. Make sure that you center the lid on the box so that there is equal overhang all around. See Fig 3.

Paint the outside, the edges, the bottom, and the inside of the lid with beige enamel. It may require several coats if the cardboard is very absorbent.

While your box is drying, lay out the shells on your paper patterns as it is essential to have a basic plan of arrangement in mind before you start gluing.

Start with the lid and arrange a border of one type of shell all around the perimeter. Ours were ¼" white clam shells, but any small, relatively flat shells will do as well. They should be of a color to contrast with the shells used as fillers. Next arrange the center motif; a cluster of single specimens or a matched pair of scallops or mussel shells is attractive.

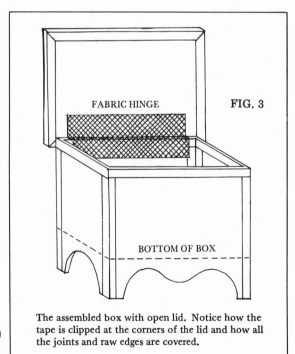

FABRIC HINGE   FIG. 3

BOTTOM OF BOX

The assembled box with open lid. Notice how the tape is clipped at the corners of the lid and how all the joints and raw edges are covered.

allow it to dry and then turn the box over and glue the shells on the front. (A 12" square of 1" foam rubber to lay the box on while you work prevents damage to the shells that have already been glued.) When you have glued the shells on all four sides and they are dry, set the box on its feet and decorate the top. When the top is dry give the entire box a coat of clear acrylic spray finish.

To line the box and finish it off nicely, you may use either a fancy paper or fabric. Whichever you decide upon, the procedure is the same. Using lightweight cardboard, cut two rectangles along the broken lines of each lining pattern (see Fig. 4). This will give you six pieces. Next cut two pieces of lining material (fabric or paper) from each pattern along the *solid* lines. Fold back the flaps along the broken lines. Cover all six of the cardboard rectangles with lining material, gluing down the flaps on the wrong side. If you wish to use the box for jewelry, use a soft silky fabric for lining and pad each piece of cardboard with a piece of lightweight flannel before covering.

Cut a strip of lining material 3" wide and 5" long. Turn under enough on each end so that it just covers the cotton hinge and fix it in place with a line of glue at top and bottom, leaving it loose over the hinge. Apply the glue sparingly so that it does not stain the fabric. Now spread glue on the backs of the side linings and fix them in place. Next glue in the front and back linings and lastly the bottom and lid lining.

Cassell has some further suggestions for objects to be embellished with shells.

The figure of an ancient Greek temple, the Colosseum, museum obelisk, or ancient castle, either with clock-face or without, may be easily constructed and adorned with shells, so as to produce an elaborate and effective ornament.

It should be observed that the appearance of all such ornaments is greatly improved by their being set under a glass shade, which lends a luster to them, and at the same time prevents their being handled. A common mantel-shelf clock, bought at a clockmaker's, may be adorned with advantage by this means, so as to render it a handsome ornament. The smallest kind of shells may well be used for the purpose of decking small wooden toys, which will render them well suited as appendages to the drawing-room whatnot. An especially useful purpose to which shells may be applied is the decoration of stands for baskets of sea-weed, grasses, or imitation fish. The underpart of the baskets where the sea-weeds are arranged may also be decorated with shells.

The manufacture of shell toilette boxes and pincushions might afford great amusement to visitors at the sea-side.

Chipped or damaged glass or china toilette-bottles or baskets may be restored by rubbing them over with emery paper, to take off the smoothness of the surface, and decking them with shells.

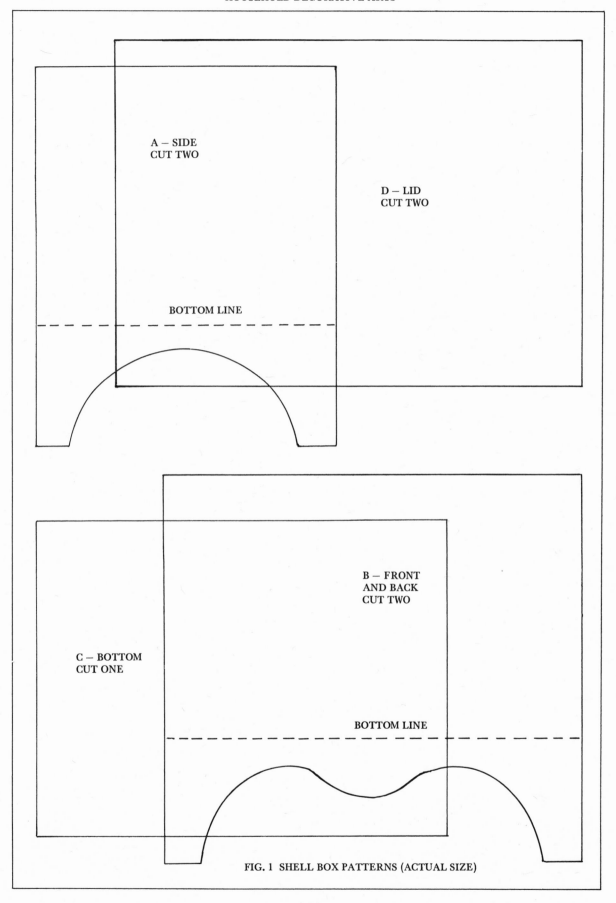

A – SIDE
CUT TWO

D – LID
CUT TWO

BOTTOM LINE

B – FRONT
AND BACK
CUT TWO

C – BOTTOM
CUT ONE

BOTTOM LINE

FIG. 1 SHELL BOX PATTERNS (ACTUAL SIZE)

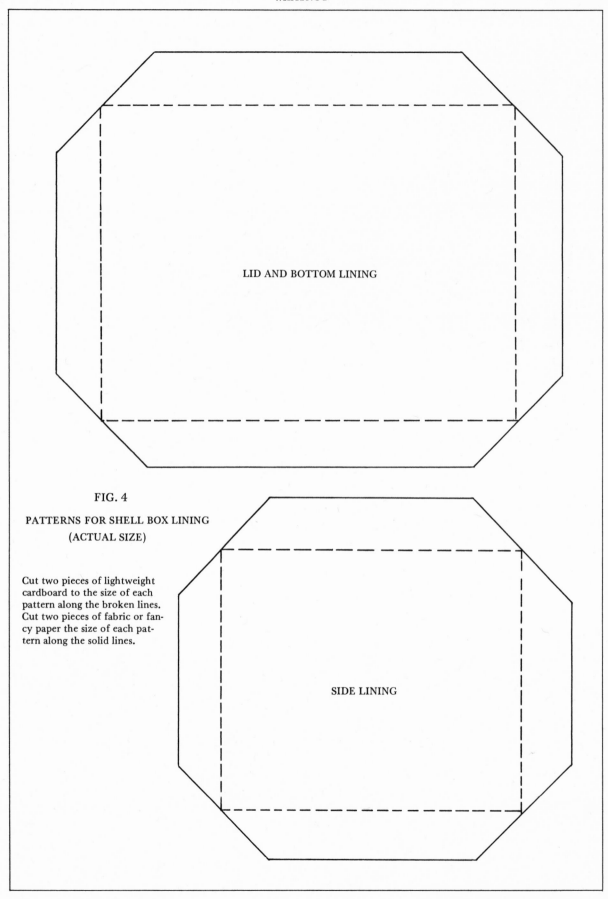

FIG. 4

PATTERNS FOR SHELL BOX LINING
(ACTUAL SIZE)

Cut two pieces of lightweight
cardboard to the size of each
pattern along the broken lines.
Cut two pieces of fabric or fancy paper the size of each pattern along the solid lines.

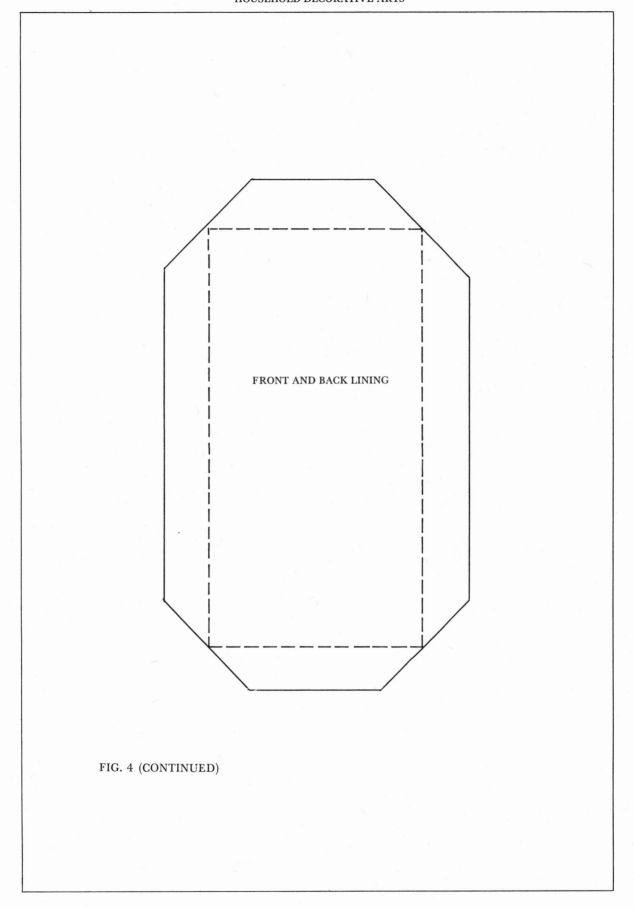

FRONT AND BACK LINING

FIG. 4 (CONTINUED)

A bouquet of fanciful, hand-painted shell flowers in a wicker basket.

Shell Flowers

If any one parlor ornament could be said to typify the Victorian taste, surely it would be the vase of shell flowers, usually carefully dust-proofed with a glass shade and reposing grandly on a red velvet stand. Some of these confections attained monumental proportions. But we were particularly taken with Cassell's charming little flower basket and tried to reproduce it as faithfully as possible.

In the basket will be observed on the left a passion-flower, lilies of the valley, and some other flowers; on the right, a dahlia, a small ranunculus, and part of a rose. In the center of the basket, which is engraved from a photo-graph, is a damask rose; on the reverse side are a yellow rose, a large ranunculus, and China aster, crocuses, and snowdrops, and the basket is complete with rosebuds, cineraria, geranium, a camellia, fuchsias — in short, all the flowers here shown with buds and leaves. The leaves are the ordinary muslin ones, such as are employed for bonnets. The shells are very brittle, but with proper security from injury, they will last more than one generation.

You will need:

Shells
White glue
Cotton wadding
Artist's acrylic paints

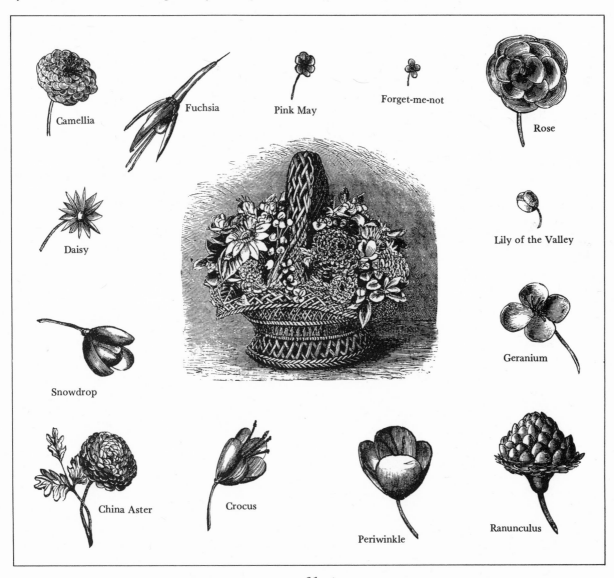

Camellia
Fuchsia
Pink May
Forget-me-not
Rose
Daisy
Lily of the Valley
Snowdrop
Geranium
China Aster
Crocus
Periwinkle
Ranunculus

Plastic kitchen wrap
Galvanized wire, 18 guage
Florist's tape
Artificial leaves and calyxes
Small fancy basket
Heavy metal, needle-type flower holder
Rubber bands
Ten to twelve jelly glasses or jars
Needle-nose pliers
Plaster of paris

Cover the tops of a number of jars with plastic wrap, indenting it slightly to form a shallow basin. You may have to hold the plastic wrap in place with rubber bands.

Sort your shells according to size, and experiment with them by laying them out in flower shapes.

Saturate a wad of cotton with white glue and put it in the center of one of the basins. Starting with the larger outside petals, press the shells into the cotton. Depending on the type of flower you are forming, your shells may overlap or not, but make sure every one is well seated in the glued cotton. If your flower has many layers of petals, you may want to add more cotton half way through the building process. Allow the flowers to dry in the glasses so that they hold their cupped shape.

Cut wire stems approximately 12" long, and using your needle-nose pliers, coil one end (see Fig. 1) to hold the flower heads. The coil creates a kind of cup. Put a wad of glued cotton into this cup and attach a flower head. Dry the flowers upside down, on the table. (see Fig. 2).

When dry, slip a calyx up the stem until it covers the wire cup, then, starting just below the calyx, wrap the stem with florist's tape, inserting leaves as desired.

If most of your shells are white, you will want to add some color to the bouquet. We found that very pale pastels produced the most effective contrast with the natural shell colors.

Use acrylic colors, mixed with a great deal of white, to paint the finished flowers. Leave a great many white ones, as they add sparkle to the finished arrangement.

Use a heavy metal, needle-type flower holder to make your arrangement. Line the bottom of the basket with plastic wrap, place the arranged flowers in it, and pour wet plaster of paris in around the holder and deep enough to embed the bottoms of the stems. When it dries, the arrangement will be securely fastened and the plaster will provide enough weight to prevent the basket from overturning.

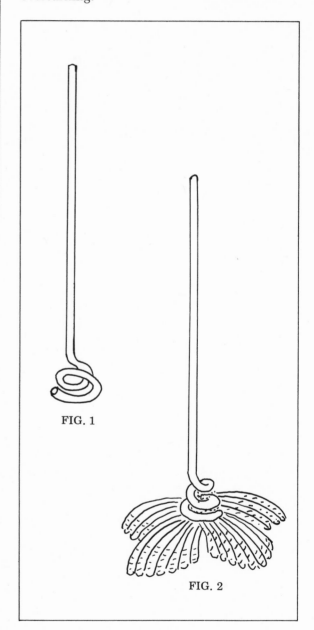

FIG. 1

FIG. 2

Decoration in Imitation Marble

Glass decoration is capable of being used for or as an imitation of marble, and as such may be employed for the tops of tables, or for the panels of pilasters, &c., in chimney-pieces. In representing marble upon glass, it is necessary that the veins should be first painted in, as these will require to be very delicately drawn. It will be well for the decorator to lay the plate of glass over paper of the same color as the marble to be imitated, which will thus enable him to see the exact nature of his lines. Where distinct veins are desired, the lines should be allowed to become dry before the general color of the marble is painted in; in others, where, as in Sicilian, they have a misty appearance, the general color should be painted on while they are still somewhat wet, and the effect of their melting into it will thus be gained. The effect of spots may be given by spurting color from the brush. Malachite is imitated by, in the first instance, taking a little black paint, very much thinned, and working it round with the tip of the finger, so as to form concentric rings, and then painting it over with emerald green. The imitation of marble upon glass is not, however, always successfully practiced by an unprofessional operator, and this design will be much more easily carried out in the second method, which is by merely laying in the different parts in flat colors, which at a little distance has an almost equally good effect. . . .

The colors have to be applied on that side which is intended to be farthest from the spectators, and that those colors or ornaments which are to show most prominently are to be applied first.

This is a simple and effective way to redecorate a table or dresser top, especially if you want a temporary change that can be done quickly and is fun to do. All you need is a piece of glass cut to the right size and some artist's acrylic paints. One of the advantages of acrylic paint is that if you don't like the effect you've just created you can wash it off before the paint is dry and start again. If you want your imitation to be realistic, try to find colored photographs of some marble to copy; if not, use your imagination.

Decide on the basic color of your marble and mix three or four variations of it by adding white or graying it slightly with black. Mix enough of each variation so that you can work quickly once you start to paint and will not need to stop to mix more paint.

Lay in the veins with black, slightly softened with white, and some of the color of your marble. Make some of them wider and darker and some more narrow and light. Now, before the veins are completely dry, paint the areas in between, varying the background color as you go. Some of the veins will fade into the background and some will stay bright and clear and look very similar to real marble.

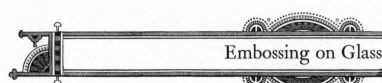

Embossing on Glass

This is Cassell's quaint name for etching glass, and can be a very effective way of blocking an unattractive view, covering clear glass for privacy, or of adding a decorative border to a plain glass-fronted cabinet. Glass embossing is so easy to do that one has to resist the temptation to embellish every pane of glass in the house.

You will need:

Glass etching compound (available at stained glass suppliers and some hobby shops)
Plain, light-colored adhesive-backed shelf lining paper (such as Contact)
Carbon paper
X-Acto knife, fine tip
Rubber gloves
Cotton swabs or an old paint brush

Measure the area to be decorated. Draw your design on paper, then, using commercial carbon paper, transfer it to the adhesive-backed paper. Apply the paper design to the glass surface. (If it is possible to lay the glass flat on a table, so much the better.) Now, using a fine razor knife, cut away the portions of the design that are to be etched. Be sure to cut even, clear lines; the pieces may then be lifted out with the tip of the knife. It is possible, with a little practice, to cut quite intricate details.

When all the cutting is finished, go over the design to make sure that all the edges of the adhesive-backed paper are adhering tightly to the glass and that all areas not to be etched, including any wood frames, are protected.

Cover your work area with newspapers in case of spills. Put on rubber gloves and stir the etching compound until well mixed. Apply the compound with cotton swabs or an old paint brush. Daub it on rather heavily (or follow the instructions that come with the etching compound). The compound will take away the surface of the exposed glass, thereby creating a design. After approximately forty-five minutes, wash the glass well with warm water (or as directed on the label) and remove the adhesive-backed paper. Wash again to get any residue off the glass.

Do be careful with the etching compound; any acid strong enough to take the surface off glass will take the surface off your hands as well.

There is a spray-on glass frosting on the market that can be used in the same way, and can be scraped off if desired.

DESIGNS FOR EMBOSSING ON GLASS

An ornate embossed (etched) glass panel for a door
or window.

Potichomanie

The beautifully painted vases of Indian and Chinese workmanship, which adorn the homes of the wealthy, are generally very expensive, not unfrequently costing hundreds of pounds each. Indeed, Frederick the Great of Prussia is recorded to have received from one of his brother potentates a whole regiment of guards in exchange for a single pair of porcelain vases. But articles almost, sometimes quite, equal in effect, though, of course, without merit of being genuine, may be made by any person, with the outlay of a little labor and good taste, from jars or other articles of plain glass, by the aid of the art of potichomanie.

A POTICHE

It was a polite fiction of the era that all properly reared young ladies were artistic and could draw and paint with skill. Of course, it wasn't always true, so any means of "artistic expression" that didn't require much real talent was enthusiastically received. Just such a technique was offered by potichomanie, a method of decorating vases. The word derives from the French — "potiche: vase" — and from the Greek — "mania: madness."

Potiche

You will need:

Clear-glass container, such as a cookie jar or vase, with a fairly wide neck
Pictures — oriental motifs are appropriate (we used an old calendar with reproductions of Japanese art)
Gloss découpage finish
Semigloss oil base enamel paint

Pick out a paint color that is appropriate for fine porcelain, such as grayed white or soft celedon.

Plan the layout of your design and carefully cut out the motifs. Fingernail scissors are helpful. Be sure to cut off all of the background color so there will be a well-defined edge to each part of the design.

Paint a thin coat of découpage finish on the inside of the glass and position the cutout motifs on it, face down, so the right side of the picture shows through the glass. Press the design down carefully, working out any air bubbles. You can check from the outside of the container to make sure that the paper is adhering smoothly. Let the first coat dry thoroughly, then apply a second coat covering the entire inside of the container.

When the découpage finish is dry, paint the inside of the container with an even coat of the enamel you have chosen. If there is any shading or unevenness in the paint, give it a second coat. Paint right over the cutouts.

These containers will not hold up as flower vases unless you use a separate container for water. Nor should they be used for unwrapped food storage. But they do make charming potpourri jars.

Ornamental Jardinières

The current craze for house plants is nothing new. They were every bit as popular in Victoria's day. Ordinary clay pots would have looked positively naked sitting, unadorned, in the parlor, and Cassell offers any number of ways to conceal them with pretty covers. We made several such covers, and they are a very attractive way to gift wrap a plant. The Etrusco-Egyptian pots are particularly amusing — though one may suspect the authenticity of the designs. But be it Egyptian, Etruscan, or Grecian, no one can dispute their obvious air of antiquity.

Imitation Sèvres China and Wedgwood

Very pretty jardinières may be made in imitation of these styles. Each jardinière is cut out of cardboard wide enough to hold the flowerpot and saucer, and an inch higher than the top of the pot. Cut the sides in four pieces, of stout white cardboard narrower at the base by an inch than at the top. Join the four pieces by strips of thin linen, pasted inside, down the corners. When these are dry, line the inside with good white paper [that is, glue the paper to the inside]. *Let this also dry. Then take four pieces of turquoise-blue paper, cut to the size of the sides. Cut out and remove an oval shape from the center of each one and paste neatly on each side of the jardinière. Next, with purchased German embossed garlands* [or cut out small, brightly colored flower pictures from magazines or greeting cards], *ornament the edges of the ovals, disguising the meeting of the blue and white paper. One or two tiny cupids and butterflies, or little birds, may be introduced into these garlands. The top edges should be covered with a narrow strip of*

FIG. 1

FIG. 2

FIG. 3

IMITATION SÈVRES CHINA AND WEDGWOOD DESIGNS

gold paper, and a border of flowers should be glued all round above and below the oval decorations. See Fig. 1. The Sevigne Sèvres china is imitated in the blue paper; for Du Barry china, substitute pink.

The Wedgwood jardinières are made of cardboard in the same manner, except the paper covering and lining them should be of a matte finish, and in a color resembling Wedgwood blue or green. Cut out the embossed designs from white lace paper — figures are the best — and attach with gum to the center of each side of the jardinière. Glue the level parts of the figure, not the raised ones, and be sure not to flatten it in pressing it on. Edge the top with white paper, instead of gold. Fig. 2 illustrates the Wedgwood jardinière. Fig. 3 presents a pretty design for a long narrow window box.

Natural Flowerpot Covers

The most elegant of flowerpot covers can be made with materials furnished by the hand of nature. Lavender from the garden, corn, barley, or oats make very pretty flower-

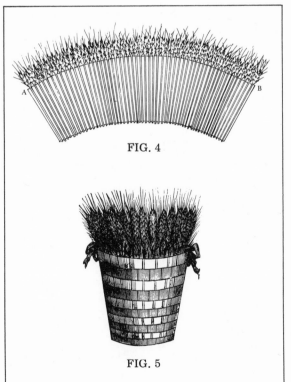

FIG. 4

FIG. 5

pot covers when woven together with new, bright-green satin ribbon. A bow looks pretty put on each side like handles.

You will need:

Flowerpot, 6½"
Fifty to sixty stalks of natural material
Heavy paper, 16" square
Ribbon, 6½ yards of ¾" wide
Masking tape, ½" wide
Rubber cement

Cut a curved piece of heavy paper that will just cover the flowerpot with a 1" overlap. This paper is a pattern and will not be used in the finished cover. Tape the pattern flat on your worktable. Arrange the stalks of natural material in close, even rows over the pattern, with the flower or grain heads protruding above the top edge. Cut the stems even along the bottom edge of the pattern (see Fig. 4).

Hold the stalks in place with a long piece of paper stretched tightly over the heads and taped to the table at each end.

Now starting at A, Fig. 4, weave a length of ribbon, right side down, in and out among the stems just under the flower heads and following the curve of the pattern. Cut the ribbon at B, Fig. 4, and lightly tape it in place at both ends. Starting at side A again weave a second row of ribbon, going over and under alternate stalks. Cut and tape as before, and so on, until the entire pattern is covered with woven ribbon.

Run a line of masking tape along the bottom ribbon to hold the stalks even, making sure that the tape does not show on the right side. Run a line of tape down sides A and B, Fig. 4, to hold all of the loose ribbon ends and trim the edges even.

Remove the pot cover from the pattern, and glue the edges together along the A and B lines. Make two small perky bows of the remaining ribbon and sew one on each side as shown in Fig. 5.

Flowerpot Stands

These stands are made of old cigar-boxes; if the box is a square one, which is sometimes the case, so much the better; but if not, the

DESIGN FOR A FLOWERPOT STAND

box is easily pulled to pieces, the thin board of which it is composed cut to the required size, the parts fastened together again with brads, and the corners new bound by pasting strips of gilt or colored paper over them. As shown in our illustration [above], the stand may also be improved in appearance by gluing four small balls of turned wood upon the corners, the lower ones to serve as feet.

The unpolished mahogany of which cigar-boxes are made, forms a very agreeable background to this method of decoration. Holes are bored through the sides of the box with a gimlet, and through these holes Berlin wool is worked with a needle. In this manner a great variety of rectilinear patterns may be formed; all others being, of course, impossi-

ble; and by selecting the colors with judgement admirable effects may be produced. It is usual to conceal the larger holes by small rosettes of yarn, fastening them on the inner side.

Etrusco-Egyptian Flowerpots

The fashion, now so general, of using growing plants as ornaments for the dinner table has led to the manufacture of various baskets and vases, some of silver and some of china, in which to place them so as to conceal the flowerpot, which would be somewhat unsightly if left uncovered. By those who do not possess either silver or china vases, the Etrusco-Egyptian flowerpot, of which we give an illustration, will be found a simple and pretty substitute. A common flowerpot must be selected, of sufficient size to allow that in which the plant is growing to stand within it. Some Egyptian designs, such as those shown, are painted upon the flowerpot, with a fine camel-hair brush, in ivory-black. The best way of doing it is to place the flowerpot on its side, with a heavy book on each side to keep it steady, and, bringing it near the edge of the table, to use a painter's resting-stick to steady the hand, as the designs should be steadily and sharply done. The saucer should be ornamented in like manner. It is found that

DESIGNS FOR ETRUSCO-EGYPTIAN
FLOWERPOTS

a larger design for the center and smaller ones dotted over the plain ground, have a better effect than if subjects all the same size be used, as they bear a closer resemblance to the vases which they are intended to imitate. Any illustrated work on Egypt will give a variety of figures and animals suitable for the purpose.

Cardboard Fretwork Covers

Pretty ornaments can be made for flowerpots by cutting out white cardboard. Fig. 6 is a very good design for the purpose. It is a fleur-de-lis, the common flag-flower of our country streams. Trace the shape of the panel, of a size to cover the pot, on a large sheet of cardboard. Cut four panels the same. Draw the design on each panel, and cut out with a sharp knife. On the clearness of the cutting depends the beauty of the ornament. In Fig. 6, the upright spear, with its bulb center, is left standing in cardboard in the midst of the excavation. Line all the open parts at the back with colored paper, silk or satin. Join the four finished panels together by glued strips of paper inside at each corner. The Gothic tops of the ornaments should be entirely above the flowerpot, and only the lowest parts of the card level with the top of the pot. Figs. 7, 8, and 9 are more complicated designs, requiring greater care and skill in their execution. The entire outlines are cut out, and the markings and shadings are painted on the lining of colored paper or fabric.

FIG. 8

FIG. 7

FIG. 9

FIG. 6

Point Lace Work

Victorians made this type of imitation lace with what was called point lace braid. It is hard to find such braid nowadays, but we have experimented with regular insertion-type lace and it works very well. The possibilities for point lace work are limited only by the imagination of the worker, as it can be made large and bold in scale or very fine and delicate, depending on the size of the braid and the gauge of the thread. The Victorian ladies used point lace for collars, parasol covers, handkerchief borders, bonnets, in fact, for anything that could be decorated with or made of, lace.

Cassell begins his commentary on point lace by waxing philosophic.

The longer we live in this world the more we find that there is indeed nothing new under the sun, and each successive day only brings us back to the works and devices of our ancestors.

It is even so with the employments, or rather amusements, in which ladies spend their hours of leisure from more important occupations; and the point lace, on which so much time was spent in days when it was used for ecclesiastical purposes, as well as for every ornamental part of women's dress, has again become a fashionable pursuit, many a female finger being now busy in imitating, although it cannot excel, the handiwork of those long since gathered to their fathers.

The materials required for point lace are not many nor expensive, being some pink glazed calico, some strong paper, several yards (say a dozen) of point lace braid, some fine linen thread, and a large needle. Trace out your design on the calico and sew it to a piece of strong paper so as to ensure the flatness and firmness of both. The pink
color enables the worker to see the pattern more easily by gaslight.*

The braid employed may be of two kinds, the plain, with an open edge, A, in Fig. 1 or one with a round opening at intervals in the center, B, in Fig. 1, giving a more decidedly lace-like appearance to the work. To avoid joining which is very important, the braid should be wound double on a card, leaving the two ends to commence the work with; by this means, cutting is avoided. The braid must be carefully [basted on along its outer edge] taking the stitches (of which there should not be too many) quite through both calico and paper, and following the design in all its meanderings as exactly as possible. In those places where the design is pointed great care should be taken to keep it as flat as possible at the point and the braid should be folded and kept to the shape in turning it with much nicety. The outside edge must exactly follow the line, the stitches being taken through the pattern, keeping the braid well strained, and sewing it over to prevent its widening where sharp turns are required. When the outer edge is done, the inner one

FIG. 1

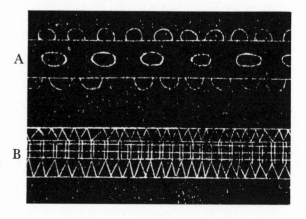

must be attended to, and this must be gathered in to fit each turn, as, owing to its width, it will necessarily be much fuller on the inside of a curve than on the outside. A needle with fine thread must therefore be passed along this side of the braid, taking a small stitch over it, as in whipping a frill; and by means of this thread the braid may be drawn to fit the various curves of the design. Great care must be taken that this gathering thread be not in any place sewn through the material on which the pattern is traced; it must be neatly done on the surface only as it cannot be touched again, and remains in when the work is completed.

When the whole design has been braided, the outside edge of the braid has an open stitch worked into it, which we will call the "open over-cast," and it is thus accomplished: With fine thread the needle must be passed through one of the openings in the edging of the braid, as if for over-casting, but the stitch must not be drawn tighter than is required to make it about the same size as the edging of the braid, then the needle being passed through the single part of the stitch still in the manner of over-casting, the thread is drawn tightly and fastens the stitch; this double over-cast is repeated on the inside of the braid. With this over-cast a great deal may be done toward making the braid lie well to the pattern; in the curves for instance — where the inner edge will naturally be slightly fuller than the outer, or vice versa — by omitting one or two stitches of open-work, in one case, or putting two stitches into one, in the other, it will be made right. It is almost needless to add that in the braiding only must the needle be taken through the calico and paper, all the rest of the work must be done on the surface, and care must be taken not to catch up the calico with it.

Next, all the open portions of the design must be filled up with fancy stitches, and of these there is such a variety as almost to baffle description. However, we will attempt to particularise some, and hope, with the aid of the designs, to make them tolerably intelligible.

POINT DE BRUXELLES

This is formed with successive rows of buttonhole stitches. Start on the right in a corner and make a loop across the space; return by making a loose buttonhole stitch into the first loop, and so form two loops. For each row, fill every loop of the previous row with a loose buttonhole stitch. Fig. 2 shows the stitch being made from left to right and Fig. 3 shows it being made from right to left.

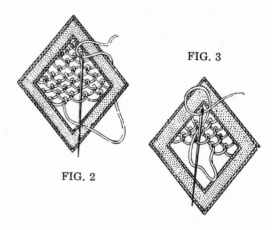

FIG. 3

FIG. 2

POINT D'ESPAGNE

Start to work from the left side of the opening. Put the needle into the braid at the top of the opening and bring it out inside the loop made by the thread. Draw it up rather loosely and pass the needle again under the stitch, and make the next loop in the same manner, and so on until you reach the right hand side. Return by overcasting into each space. Work the next row in the same manner, making a loop into every space. [See Fig. 4.]

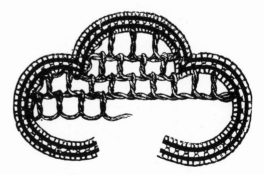

FIG. 4

TREBLE POINT D'ESPAGNE

First row work three close stitches and one wide alternately. Second row work three close stitches into the open space, and one long loop below the three close stitches, and so on . [See Fig. 5.]

FIG. 5

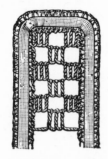

POINT D'ESPAGNE AND POINT BRUXELLES

Fig. 6 shows the manner of filling by working these two stitches alternately. Work three rows of Point de Bruxelles and then one of Point d' Espagne and so on.

FIG. 6

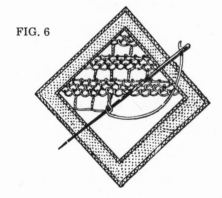

POINT DE BRABANCON

Start on the left side and work one long and one small buttonhole stitch in succession to the end of the row. Second row work seven close buttonhole stitches into the long and two loose stitches into the small loops. Repeat the rows alternately. [See Fig. 7.]

FIG. 7

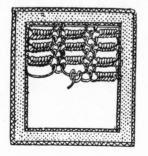

POINT D' ANGLETERRE

Fill up the space with single threads at an equal distance apart first in one direction and then in the other at right angles. Then make diagonal lines and at the place where they intersect each other make one overcast to keep the threads together. The needle and thread are passed under and over the threads until a tiny wheel is formed, and after which the thread is proceeded diagonally to the next intersecting point, where a wheel is again worked and so on. [See Fig. 8 and 9.]

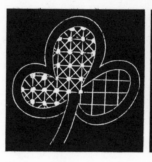
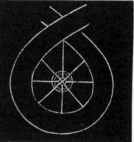

FIG. 8   FIG. 9

The bars joining the various parts of the design are done when all the filling up is completed. To make them, the needle with fine thread, after being darned in and out of the center of the braid to make the end secure, is brought out at the edge and passed across three or four times to the opposite opening, and upon these threads a close buttonhole stitch is worked for about four or five stitches, then a loose buttonhole stitch is made. Pass the needle several times through the loop and pull tight, forming a dot. Continue to the other side making close buttonhole stitches. On reaching the end of the bar, the thread worked with may be fastened off in the braid, or carefully darned along it until the next bar is reached. In those parts of the design where the braid on one side comes very near to that on the other, the braids may be drawn together by passing the needle from one to the other.

The threads holding the braiding must be cut when all is finished, and the work taken off with the greatest of care.

FIG. 10

PATTERN FOR HANDKERCHIEF BORDER Cassell's design shows only the braiding and bars. The needle worker must fill in the open spaces with a variety of stitches of her or his own choosing.

The learner will find that, after a little practice, she will be able to invent patterns of her own, suitable in size and character to the place they are intended to decorate. The opporturnity which lace-work thus affords for the exercise of individual ingenuity and taste is certainly not the least of its recommendations.

Designs for a Sofa Cushion

This design for a sofa cushion in point lace will be found very effective and convenient to work. It is done in separate squares with rather fine point lace braid. To make the cushion, a pillow of ticking, eighteen inches square, stuffed with feathers must be made and covered with crimson velvet. This being completed the squares of lace stitched together in diagonal rows, must be tacked on to it, and so as to alternate the squares of lace and plain velvet, as shown in Fig. 11. We have given two designs for the squares Fig. 12 and 13 which may be alternated. A thick crimson cord should be sewn around the edge of the cushion, and handsome tassels placed at the corners.

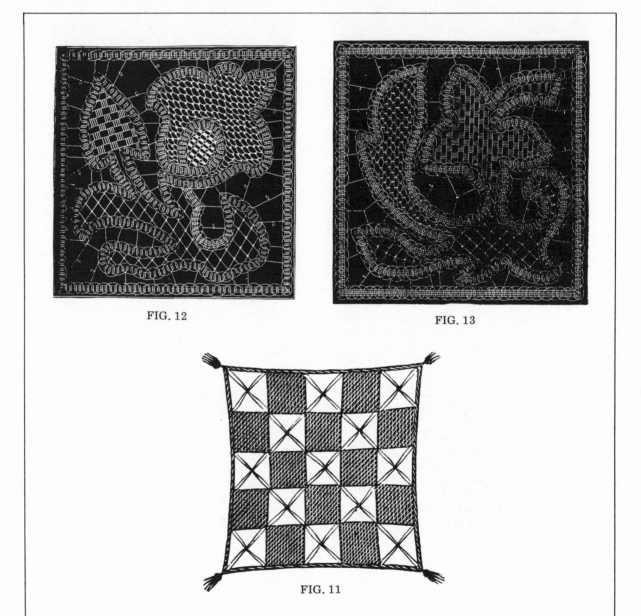

FIG. 12

FIG. 13

FIG. 11

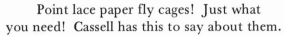

Point Lace Paper Fly Cages

Point lace paper fly cages! Just what you need! Cassell has this to say about them.

Point lace paper fly cages are really elegant little things in their way, and one can readily be made from a model, with a moderate amount of patience, in an evening.

We made one of these dainty frivolities, and found that it did indeed take patience — and slightly more than a moderate amount! The best plan of action is to build a roaring fire on the hearth, set your son to roasting chestnuts, your daughter to stitching her sampler, and then, while your spouse reads aloud from *David Copperfield,* you snip away on a fly cage. When you have exhausted the collected works of Dickens, you should have enough cages to decorate a Christmas tree, and the result will be enchanting.

Cut eight pieces like Fig. 1 out of thin, crisp, white paper, and eight like Fig. 2. The best way is first to pencil the outline, and then cut the paper. With a little skill, enough may be cut at once by folding the paper.

We used fingernail scissors and cut four at a time.

The design and the border, be it observed, must all be kept in one, and in no place are the lines to be cut through, only the spaces between to be cut out with a very sharp knife, and the paper laid on stout cardboard. The dotted lines are the pieces by which the lace is to be joined to make the cage. Take the full measure from A to B, Fig. 1, and cut a circle, the diameter of which is double that size. With a compass this is very easy. Without that aid, a tumbler or small basin may serve to draw the round. Cut it out of thin cardboard and cover it both sides with green paper.

If the cages are intended as Christmas ornaments, you could use gold or red paper to vary the color of the circles.

Divide [the circle] *into eight equal sections with a pencil line, as Fig. 3, on each side. Make a hole exactly in the center just large enough to insert a wire. Make two loops in this to keep the round in its place, one above and one below the round. The wire must be left long enough below the round of card to hold eight pieces of Fig. 2 and a tassel. Above, it must be as long as Fig. 1. Now, at the top of the round, glue the eight pieces of Fig. 1 upright from C to A to the wire. The dotted piece from A to B is glued and fastened to the round. Fix the lower part of each piece of lace, one on each pencil line on the round. Apply glue to both parts of the piece of lace before attaching it to the wire and round. Next attach the eight pieces of Fig. 2 below the round to the wire in the center, and at the top to the eight sections previously penciled on the round.*

The piece which projects from Fig. 1 requires a bit of very fine wire run through it from B to E to keep it out in place beyond the round of cardboard. The best way to do this is to cut four pieces of wire as long as the round of card is across, and as long as two of the projecting pieces of lace, leaving a little bit to turn down each side [by "turn down," Cassell means make a loop]. *Turn down one end, run the wire through the lace from end to end, and turn down the opposite end to prevent its slipping out. This wire should not show. There are some little holes from B to E for its insertion.*

At the bottom of the fly cage fix a long tassel of tissue paper; cut this like Fig. 4, leaving enough plain for a heading. Tie the top to the wire below close to the lace, wrong way up, like Fig. 5, then turn it down. Tie it a second time, above the fringed ends, like Fig. 6. It should be put on before the lace.

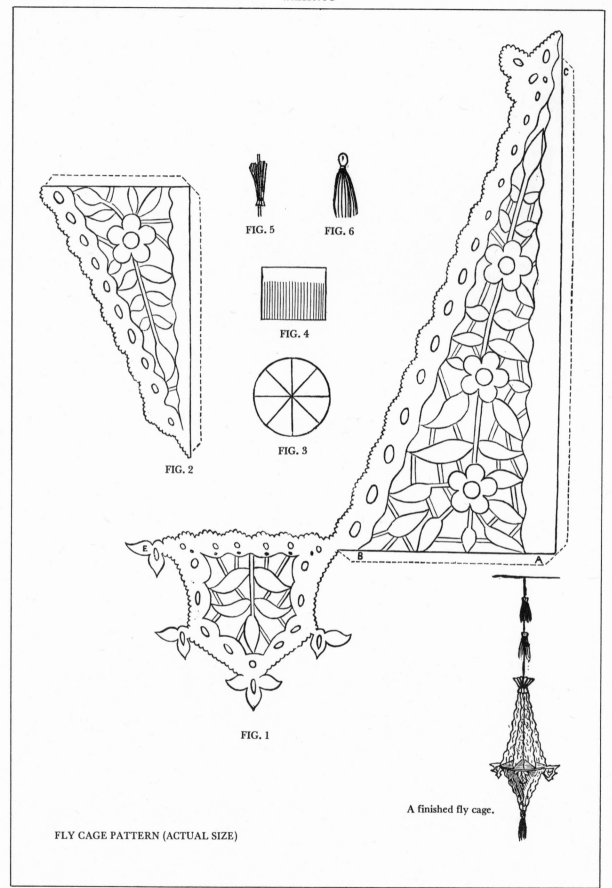

FIG. 5

FIG. 6

FIG. 4

FIG. 3

FIG. 2

FIG. 1

A finished fly cage.

FLY CAGE PATTERN (ACTUAL SIZE)

Beadwork

Cassell's marvelous beaded sideboard (below) conjures up pictures of the children gathered round the tea-table on some rare occasion of escape from the nursery, listening, wide-eyed, to the fables of Aesop as illustrated on this alarming tribute to creative endeavor.

Bead Mosaic

Bead mosaic differs from ordinary bead-work in this respect — that the beads, instead of being sewn upon canvas, or some other textile fabric, are fastened by cement to some hard and firm background, such as one composed of wood or metal.

All descriptions of glass beads may be used for this art, except perhaps, those of extremely large size and of eccentric shapes, the different ordinary sizes and shapes being applicable to different positions and purposes.

Generally speaking, neatly rounded beads are those most appropriate; but in some parts of the work, as, for instance, where perfectly straight lines have to be represented, those mere pieces of glass tubing, cut in lengths, and known as "bugles," may be found serviceable, and time will be economised by using them. Beads of as many different colors as possible should be provided. If gold beads which are thickly gilt with genuine metal can be procured, they will be of great value for enriching the work.

The groundwork on which to lay the beads may be of either wood or metal, or the mosaic may be applied to evenly plastered walls. It will in all cases be necessary that a rim, as of wood, or a gilt moulding, should surround the space to be filled, to give support to the mosaic, and prevent its being displaced by accidents.

The ground being prepared, the design is drawn or traced upon it. Any design, originally intended for Berlin wool-work can be reproduced by this art; but bead mosaic is more easily adapted to pictorial effect than is wool-work, and almost any illuminated design, ornamental border, or even picture, may be imitated in it with considerable fidelity.

The subjects most easily worked in bead mosaic are those of flat character and the art is admirably adapted to the representation of heraldic devices. With pictorial subjects of flowers, it is better to deal with them in a conventional manner rather than to aim at exact representations of Nature.

Elegant enrichments for a mantelpiece, with panels of mosaic surrounding a pier-glass, may be thus formed, or the frame of a large movable looking-glass may be very beautifully decorated by means of it. To the panels of screens, sideboards, cabinets, and other articles of furniture it may also be applied, as well as to the tops of stands for tea-urns, flagons &c.

A SIDEBOARD DECORATED WITH BEAD MOSAIC

Our project for bead mosaic is in no way comparable to Cassell's sideboard; we were very modest and did only a small inset for the back of a chair, more as a test run than as a display piece. It is clear that the technique presents many really interesting possibilities for decorating furniture or accessories.

You will need:

Beads of one size, ours were approximately 1/8"
Hatpin
White glue
Graph paper with 1/8" squares
Felt pens
Clear acrylic spray finish
Linseed oil
Whiting

Draw a light outline of your design on graph paper and fill in the colors with felt pens. Seal the drawing with acrylic spray. (Our rose was copied from a Victorian Berlin-wool rug. Needlepoint or cross-stich designs are ideal for beadwork.) Glue the pattern to a cardboard or wood backing or directly on to the surface to be beaded.

Start by beading the motif first, leaving the background until last. Pick up a row, or part of a row, of beads in the correct color order on a hat pin; paint several rows of the motif with white glue and lay the beads in place by carefully slipping them off the pin. Go on to the next row and next and so on until the entire motif is beaded, then fill in the background in the same manner. This is much easier than trying to set the beads one at a time.

When the glue has dried, brush the mosaic with linseed oil letting it run down between the beads. Sprinkle the motif with a layer of whiting, rub it well into the cracks and then wipe it clean with a soft cloth.

Beadwork on Wire

When attached to a framework of wire, instead of the ordinary background of cloth or canvas, beads can be rendered applicable to a variety of decorative articles, either for *personal use, or for the mantelshelf, or the toilette table.*

For this class of work, designs of a naturalistic character, and more especially leaves and flowers, are chiefly in favor, but it will also be found well suited for carrying out geometrical patterns.

Fashion plates of the Victorian period show the most marvelous, elaborate coiffures with hair curled and braided, pouffed and padded, and, for evening, bedecked with flowers, ribbons, feathers, and ornaments like the butterfly, made of beads strung on wire (see Fig. 2). Cassell writes:

This pretty and fashionable ornament can be made of red beads, with the key beads of gold, or if worn with a dark dress with black and gold, or to suit the taste of the wearer. Many other graceful ornaments might be made for the same purpose, as for instance, feathers, fern-leaves, or the star-shaped flowers so much worn at present.

You will need:

Beads — seed or Indian, in color as desired. The Salvation Army and other second-hand shops often have very inexpensive bead necklaces that can be broken up for beadwork. If you are working with strung beads, the thin wire can be run through with the thread so that 6 or 7 beads can be picked up on the wire at one time, much easier than picking them up individually.
Light-duty steel wire, 24 guage
Brass wire, 32 guage
Needle-nose pliers with a wirecutter
Masking tape
Pushpins

To make the frame for the butterfly shown in Fig. 1: Cut a piece of the heavier wire, slightly longer than needed. Put a twist in one end, to keep the beads from escaping, then string the wire with beads, leave an inch of wire unstrung to give a little room for bending, then put a twist in the open end of the wire.

Make a paper pattern in the shape of Fig. 1, and the size you want your butterfly to be, and tape it to a small piece of board to use as a guide. Next, starting at the end of an antenna, bend the beaded wire into the butterfly shape. Use pushpins to hold the wire to the board as you shape it. With small loops of the thin wire tie wherever the beaded wires cross. Finish at the end of the outer antenna, twist the wire neatly to finish, and cut off excess.

When the frame is shaped and wired together, begin filling in the wing sections with beads strung on the fine wire; start from the outside edge and work toward the center with each succeeding row; end each row at the body as shown in Fig. 2. Attach each row of beaded wire to the previous one with loops of thin wire, fit each loop between beads as inconspicuously as possible. Keep all the rows of beads very close together. Vary the rows of color as desired.

The body of the butterfly may be worked in the same manner as the wings, or may be made of larger beads in assorted sizes that fill up the space neatly. When your butterfly is finished, wire it to a hair-clasp or a large hair-pin.

Mr. Cassell takes beadwork a giant step further with the next gorgeous creation. If you have enjoyed your initial experiment you might feel sufficiently ambitious to attempt this.

A far more elaborate work than the foregoing is the watch and jewel stand for a toilette-table, given in Fig. 3. The base from which this arises is of wood covered with a crimson velvet cushion to receive pins and brooches. The main stem is wound with amber and chocolate beads. The small tendrils are wound with gold colored silk, with amber beads cemented on them. For the leaves, dark and light green beads. For the large central flower which surrounds the watch, petals of a bright pink, with crimson central veins, will be effective, while the same colors may be applied to the two smaller flowers. These last form cups to hold any small articles, and the pistils in their centers, which are ring holders, should each be surmounted by a large amber bead. Some of the smaller stems will, at their terminations, serve as hooks from which to hang earrings, &c.

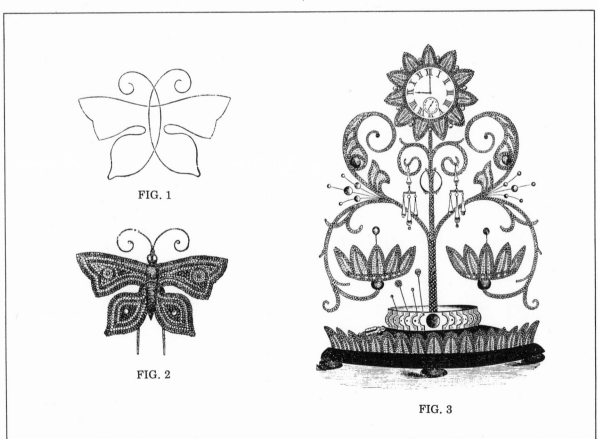

FIG. 1

FIG. 2

FIG. 3

Furniture Decorated with Chintz

Many articles of domestic furniture which have become shabby might be renovated and rendered very pretty by painting them entirely of some some effective color. When the paint is dry, decorate them with flowers and birds cut out of dimity, or colored paper scraps arranged very prettily.

Since we just happened to have some exceedingly shabby furniture stored away, we thought we would try this, and the resulting transformation was indeed "very pretty." In our case we used two inexpensive chintz patterns: a narrow, figured stripe and a floral bouquet design in similar colors, both with a Victorian look. By cutting just the narrow stripe from three yards of thirty-six inch fabric, we had the twenty-seven yards of border it took to trim a chest of drawers and a night stand. One yard of floral pattern, also thirty-six inches wide, was more than enough to provide all the flower motifs needed. In fact, there was enough of this and the border left to line the small drawer in the night stand, a very nice finishing touch. The furniture has the look of beautifully executed hand-painted pieces and, as Mr. Cassell would say, "All with no other artistic talent but taste."

Cassell's illustrations suggest the many ways you might use this form of decoration. This is how you do it.

You will need:

Semigloss, oil base enamel paint
Fabric, chintz or any lightweight, tight woven cotton (the amount depends on what you want to decorate)
Clear acrylic spray finish
Scissors
Matte découpage finish, high build up
Clear semigloss varnish
Fine waterproof sandpaper
Good-quality paintbrush

Plan your design and buy enough fabric to complete your project, maybe even a bit more than you estimated. There is nothing more frustrating than to find the store is out of your pattern when you need just a half a yard more.

When you go to get your paint, take a swatch of cloth with you to the paint store. A soft, slightly grayed, version of one of the colors in the print or a close match for the background is a safe choice. Remember that the colors on the small sample chips will always appear stronger on a large piece of furniture.

Remove all the hardware from the pieces you are going to decorate, fill any scratches, and sand the pieces thoroughly. Often a change of hardware is desirable, and this is the time to make the decision so that old holes may be filled and painted over and new ones drilled.

Give the pieces two coats of paint, sanding lightly between coats.

Spray the fabric lightly with the clear acrylic before cutting. This makes it easier to cut fine details and helps prevent the fabric from raveling. Sharp scissors are essential for this job, as you should cut very close to the lines and leave as little background attached to the motif as possible.

Paint a coat of découpage finish on the areas to be decorated and quickly apply the cutouts, then paint over the whole surface, cutouts and all. Work out any air bubbles trapped under the fabric, being careful not to fray the edges of the designs.

A small chest of drawers decorated with designs
cut from chintz.

Next, apply at least ten coats of découpage finish, letting it dry throughly each time between coats — not so tedious as it sounds as the coats dry quickly. We did find that the temperature made a great difference in the way the finish went on, so work in a heated area whenever possible.

When the tenth coat is dry, wet-sand it with very fine waterproof sandpaper until the surface is satin smooth. The water will cloud the surface, but this will clear as the finish drys. When the surface is perfectly dry again apply a coat of clear varnish as a sealer, for the découpage finish alone will water-spot.

FURNITURE DECORATED WITH CHINTZ

Leafwork on Furniture

The art of decorating cabinets, work-boxes, and other small fancy articles of wood with pressed and dried natural leaves is so old, as almost to have passed from the memory of the present generation, yet it is for many reasons well worthy of being revived. The effect produced is always pleasing, the process is simple and easy, and to those who live in the country or are accustomed to take walks in the fields, it affords an interesting pursuit, and leads to an observance of and a pleasure in the beautiful forms of the vegetable world. It consists in arranging and fastening dried leaves to the face of the wood-work in such patterns and borders as may please the fancy of the decorator. These when varnished over are permanent.

The fittest wood for decoration is pine, stained or painted. The leaves best suited to the purpose are those which are symetrical in form, and which are most pleasing in outline. Deeply serrated leaves are better than plain ovals. Very large leaves should be avoided, and even those of medium size should be used sparingly. Generally, and always for small articles, small leaves look best, and most readily combine into patterns.

The leaves may be dried in a botanist's press, but in default of such a contrivance the leaves may be prepared by laying them between blotting paper, and then placing them under a pile of books or other heavy weights; but never between the pages of a book, the moisture will discolor and eventually destroy those parts which it touches, although at the time it may not appear to injure them. Blotting paper, on account of its porous and absorbent nature, should always be used for drying.

It is well that a considerable number of leaves should be pressed before beginning to fasten them to the wood that there may be a good variety to select from; and by spreading on the table a sheet of paper as large as the surface to be decorated, and arranging the leaves upon it, it is easy to alter their positions till a pleasing pattern has been produced. They may then be affixed to the piece.

The effect of the leafwork may very frequently be increased by lines and ornamental patterns being traced upon the woodwork in gold before fastening on the leaves.

The illustrations show a work-box, a table cabinet, and a folding screen decorated by this process.

Another application of leafwork is described as:

Imitation of Japan Decoration which copies the fine lacquered pieces that were decorated in gold. For this, perfect yellow leaves are indispensable, and are to be pressed and dried in the manner already described. The piece to be decorated is given several coats of fine black paint, the leaves are then arranged and glued in place, and the whole is to be varnished.

Leafwork Desk

We had salvaged a small writing desk from the dump. It was wobbling uncertainly on three legs, and had been covered in marbelized paper that was hanging in shreds — but it had possibilities. Stripped, and with a new leg, it looked a little better, but still needed a lot of help. We tried refinishing it in the manner described in "Imitation Japan Decoration," on the theory that three coats of black paint would hid a lot of scars, and that we could paste leaves over the worst places. It turned out rather well. We used leaves from a Japanese maple, arranged in natural sprays, painted in stems and branches with metallic gold paint, and added a few wind-blown leaves where needed.

A lady's writing desk decorated in a Japanese manner with sprays of dried maple leaves.

You will need:

Satin black enamel
Sandpaper
Leaves, pressed and dried as described
Metallic gold paint
Découpage finish, or white glue
Semigloss varnish

Prepare the article for painting, and apply three coats of enamel, sanding lightly between coats. Plan the arrangement of the leaves and mark their position with light pencil marks on the black paint. Paint in the stems and branches with gold paint, then glue the leaves in place.

We used découpage finish for applying the leaves and for finishing the piece, in exactly the same way as described in "Furniture Decorated with Chintz" (see page 82).

An alternate method is to apply the leaves with white glue, let dry throughly, and finish with at least two coats of a good quality semigloss varnish, sanding lightly between coats.

If the leaves you have are very crinkled, you might experiment with pressing them gently with a steam iron. This worked very well with some leaves — but not at all with others. It's worth trying.

EXAMPLES OF LEAFWORK ON FURNITURE

Chinese Album

Nothing could be prettier or better than an album devised on the Chinese plan. . . . The merit of this book is, that it will open like a common book either way, back and front, or unfold like a panorama. It forms a pretty case for photographic portraits. Photographs of fancy subjects may be glued upon the cards and appropriate borders designed with pen and India ink; for example, around "Moses found by Pharaoh's daughter" a border of bulrushes; around heads, the outline of a mirror or a frame of beads will have a pretty effect; around the well-known subject of the Christian Martyr, a border of lilies would be appropriate.

You will need:

Ten pieces of lightweight illustration board, 5½" by 8½"
Two pieces of heavy cardboard cut to same size
Six pieces of white paper cut to same size
Two pieces of fabric, 7" by 10"
Two pieces of thin cotton batting, 5½" by 8½
Grosgrain ribbon, 3 yards of ½" wide
Watercolor or acrylic artist's paints
Clear acrylic spray finish
Razor knife
India ink
Glue

Arrange the photographs on the ten cards and lightly mark the positions on the wrong side of the cards. Draw in the shapes of the openings you will use to frame the images, (see Fig. 1) making sure that the openings are *smaller* than the pictures. Leave enough border all around to be decorated. With a sharp razor knife, cut out the shapes from the cardboard.

Border the openings with India ink or a line of color. Lightly sketch in the decorations and paint them. If you don't wish to paint your own designs, you may decorate the borders with cutouts from seed catalogues or découpage prints. Spray the decorated cards with clear acrylic finish.

Now glue the six pieces of white paper to the backs of six of the decorated cards. You should glue at the very edge of the sheets and around only three sides, leaving one long side open for insertion of the photographs.

Place four of the six backed pages face down on the table in a line about 1/8" apart and run a line of glue, top and bottom, the width of your ribbon. Cut the ribbon into two equal lengths, and firmly glue one length each to the top and bottom of the line of four cards, leaving an equal amount of ribbon free at either end.

Glue four more pages onto the backs of the first four so that the ribbon is sandwiched between. Remember to leave one long side unglued for insertion of the photo-

FIG. 1

graphs. Cover the two pieces of heavy cardboard with fabric or fancy paper. Ours are padded with thin batting, covered with sapgreen taffeta to match the ribbons, and covered again with ecru lace. These two pieces of fancily covered cardboard serve as the album's covers.

Now glue the top ribbons along the top inside of the covers. The bottom ribbons are glued halfway along the bottom, but with the end doubled back so that the free end comes out on the outside, in one case between the cover and the first page, and in the other between the back cover and the last page (see Fig. 2).

Glue the last two decorated pages to the inside covers. Fold like an accordian and tie with two bows.

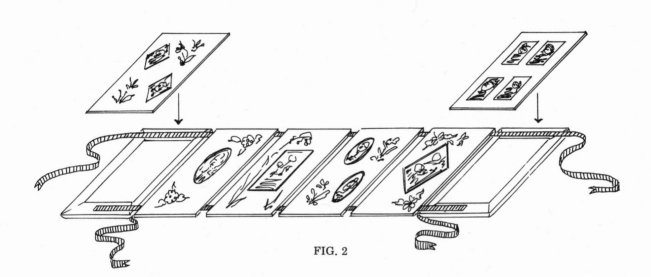

FIG. 2

Bookbinding

We have always had a yearning to try bookbinding, but the formal instructions in books on the subject were frighteningly complex and required all sorts of special tools. So we were delighted to find the following description in Cassell. Using his instructions we made a series of little books, for addresses and diaries, that are really very attractive. You can make books in almost any size, depending on their intended use.

Scrapbook

To make a scrap-book for yourself in homely style, take six sheets of paper folded one inside the other. Stitch them through the center [with carpet thread] *putting the needle in at C, taking it through A and B back to C, and knotting the two ends together, see Fig. 1. Then take another set of six sheets, and so on until you have enough for a book, stitch the whole of them through in three places, as shown in Fig. 2, first at A, knotting it together behind, then at B and at C. The book ought now to be pressed in a carpenter's press, the back upwards. Next glue the backs well, and attach three strips of linen rags* [sewing tape], *also well glued, as shown in Fig. 3. Afterwards glue the outside of them and attach the covers, in the way shown in Fig. 4. After the sides have been pressed and dried, a strip of fancy paper, or leather, or velvet is put over the back, as shown by the dotted line A, covering over the sides and corners of the covers as shown by the dotted lines B and C. These are turned down inside the covers and finished neatly. The paper or silk to cover the sides is now to be put on. The fly-leaf, or first leaf of the book ought to be nicely gummed or* *pasted down to the inside of the cover as soon as the binding is otherwise finished and dried.*

Now that your book is finished you may want to decorate the frontispiece as Cassell suggests.

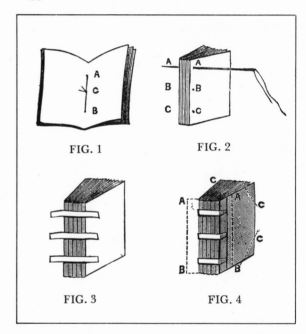

FIG. 1   FIG. 2

FIG. 3   FIG. 4

Designs for an Album Frontispiece or Cover

It used to be the fashion to ornament the fly-leaf of books for presents with marvels of flourishes and ornamentation. Like many other old customs, this has gradually fallen into disuse, but there is no reason why it should not be partially resuscitated; for very naturally the value of a present is considerably enhanced if we know and have ocular evidence of the fact that the donor spent his time in endeavouring to please. . . . We

subjoin a specimen for a beginner, which is so simple as to require but little explanation. The outline is first sketched in pencil, the black part filled in with India ink, and then shaded with sepia, and the white left blank. The outer edges [of the outline] are gone over again with a drawing pen, and the thing is done, well repaying the small amount of labor expended. See Fig. 6. Fig. 7 is another device for a cover. It represents Pandean reeds, a shepherd's pipe and crook, and a garland of roses.

Fig. 8 is a cornucopia of flowers. The cornucopia should be gold leafed and shaded with burnt umber; the flowers of varied colors — pink, yellow, damask, and blush roses, and mauve colored China-asters. . . . Relieve all the flowers and leaves by a dark shaded line underneath each, half way round. A motto, or name, may be used, according to taste.

For those who are unable to draw with colors at all, we commend another way of constructing these albums. Obtain a couple of pretty scraps, such as adorn birthday cards, and gum them one on each side of the cards which are to form the two sides of the album. If narrow wreaths of flowers can be obtained, they will serve as a pretty border.

FIG. 7

FIG. 5

FIG. 8

FIG. 6

DESIGNS FOR AN ALBUM FRONTISPIECE

Ornamental Buttonwork

This is a marvelous way to use that button collection you didn't quite know what to do with. But the designs in Cassell's *Household Guide* call for a great number of buttons which are, alas, no longer available at "2½-pence the gross." So unless you really do have a collection you want to display, you might want to simplify the design, as we did, by eliminating (in Fig. 1) the border and using only the four-button diamond design. To add interest to simpler design, we made and lined the cosy first and then sewed on the buttons, stitching them through to the lining to give an attractive quilted look.

Tea Cosies

The cosy, originally a Scotch fashion, but now almost universally adopted in England, is a useful adjunct to the breakfast table; for as it is thickly wadded and made to cover the teapot entirely, it not only keeps in the heat while the tea is infusing, but, when made, it prevents the infusion from becoming cold,

should the breakfast be a lingering meal, or be detained on account of any member of the family being less of an early riser than the rest.

The cosy should be worked on scarlet merino. [Merino is a fine wool, but other fabrics are also suitable — we used a shocking pink cotton sateen.]

In consequence of the dimensions of our publication, the pattern, Fig. 1, is necessarily given in reduced size; but the actual measurements should be, when completed, 15 inches in width by 10¼ inches in height. When the fabric has been cut to about half an inch beyond this size, a piece of white glazed lining, rather shorter at the straight edge, is put under it, and the merino tacked upon it all round, and turned over it at the straight edge. The border is now worked with the buttons, taking the stitches through to the lining; when it is finished, a small pattern of buttons is dotted, as it were, over the rest as shown. Fig. 2 or Fig. 3 may be used if preferred.

Two pieces being worked in the manner described, they must be firmly stitched to-

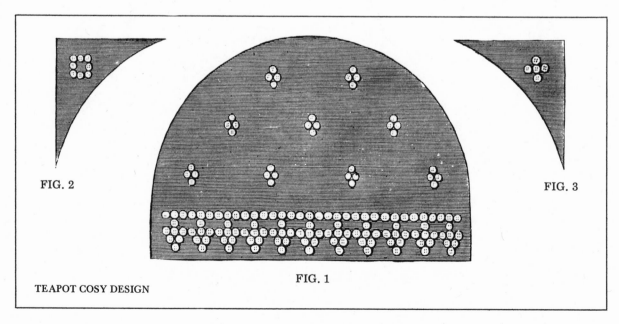

FIG. 2   FIG. 3

FIG. 1

TEAPOT COSY DESIGN

A breakfast table setting with a buttonwork tea cosy
and egg cosy. The cosies are bright pink sateen with
mother-of-pearl buttons.

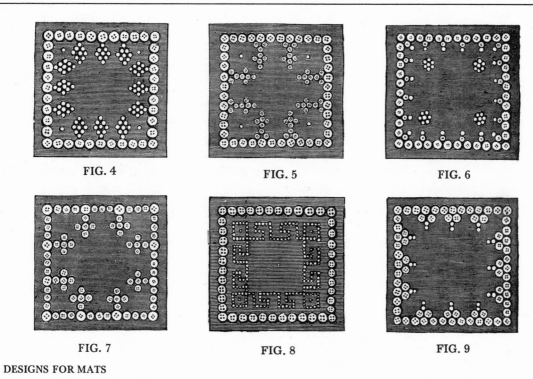

FIG. 4 FIG. 5 FIG. 6

FIG. 7 FIG. 8 FIG. 9

DESIGNS FOR MATS

gether round the curved part, on the wrong side, leaving the straight sides open. Now take a sheet of wadding [dacron batting], double it, and cut it to the shape of the cosy; cut to the same size a piece of white cotton, tack the wadding down upon it at intervals, and, having prepared two of these pieces stitch them together with the cotton on the inside. Place this inside the cosy, tacking here and there, and neatly felling down the cotton lining upon the merino, at the straight edges, on the inside.

Egg Baskets

Almost everyone knows about tea cosies, and with the growing numbers of people rediscovering the delights of drinking tea, tea cosies are more and more in evidence. But — an egg cosy? For that is what Cassell's egg basket really is. Certainly an out-of-the-ordinary item, but what a charming and unusual way to bring soft-boiled eggs, hot, to the table. And, depending on the size and shape of the basket you use, the egg cosy can be used for keeping biscuits or tortillas warm.

Another ornamental addition to the breakfast table is a basket for eggs. It should be of fine, close, fancy wickerwork, either round, oval, or, indeed, of any pretty shape, and not very deep. It may be either with or without a handle, but is more graceful and convenient for handing round, if possessing one. The basket must be well padded within with wadding, not tightly strained, and over this is placed the lining, also not tightly strained. In this basket the eggs are placed, and the wadding and lining serve to retain the heat in them until required for eating; and to ensure their being kept warm, a cover, wadded and lined, is made of the same shape as the basket, but about half an inch larger, to put over the eggs. On this cover a border may be worked in buttons, as was done with the tea-cosy.

Mats

Mats for the breakfast table may be made of sheets of common pasteboard, covered with fine French merino tacked on, leaving an inch of merino all round to turn under. A straight row of buttons is sewn all along, about half an inch from the edges, through the pasteboard and catching the turned under merino at the back. This holds the merino firmly in

place, and the tacking stitches can be removed. Finish working the design, and when completed, cover the back with white chintz with the edges turned under and sew neatly to the merino. Figs. 4 through 9 are designs for mats.

ON EGGS

Herewith, the "approved" Victorian recipe for boiling an egg. But first, a few stirring words on the wonders of eggs.

There are in this world a few common things which never fail to inspire the thoughtful mind with unceasing wonder and admiration. An egg is something which approaches the marvelous. It is neither alive nor dead, but possesses a latent vitality which may be called forth under the prescribed conditions. By consuming an egg you do not take life; you merely prevent its development. Nevertheless, this faint spark has the conservative force of actual life. An egg containing a fertile embryo will keep longer than one which has none. Harvey's grand principle, "Omne vivum ex ovo" — "Every living thing comes from an egg," has received confirmation from recent investigations. The traditions and legends respecting eggs are strange and numerous.

The very form and contour of an egg are remarkable, and most suitable for their purpose and destination, being bounded and contained in one direction by a circle, in another by an irregular ellipse. The latter curve is more elegant, because more varied than the regular oval, so called from ovum, an egg.

How many of our modern cook books rhapsodize over the ingredients they itemize? We finally come to the recipe:

EGGS BOILED IN THE SHELL. —

We feel inclined to imitate Swift's "Advice to Servants," and tell you how many ways there are of boiling eggs badly; one of which, very frequently practised, is to put them into a sauce pan without enough water to cover them. But we reserve those curious recipes for the present. There are two ways of boiling an egg well. First, drop it gently, without cracking it, into boiling water, and let it boil three minutes and a half. Secondly, drop the egg into boiling water; set the pan on the side of the stove, so as to keep hot, without ever boiling again; let the egg remain there five minutes.

Decoration of Fans — a beautiful iridescent appearance may be imparted to fans with mounts of white paper by floating a few drops of varnish on a vessel filled with water, inserting the fan beneath the surface, and gradually raising it in such a manner as to cover the paper with the thin film of varnish which will have spread over the top of the water, and then drying it.

Black and Gilded Box

The section on gilding from Cassell gave a great many instructions on applying gold leaf, but contained no specific project. We adapted several of his suggested techniques to decorate an old tin bread box. The same technique we describe here can also be used on wood or papier-mâché and can serve to decorate any object or piece of furniture not subject to hard wear.

For our design we traced a traditional wild rose pattern from Cassell, and extended the stems to frame each panel.

You will need:

Box
Gold metal leaf
Quick-drying gold size
India ink
Clear acrylic spray finish
Fine point drawing pen
Watercolor brushes, sizes 0, 2, and 4
Masking tape

Measure your box and plot your design on paper. The design can cover the whole box or just sections of the sides.

Mark the general areas which are to be gold on the box. Give these areas a thin coat of gold size. When it is almost dry, just barely tacky to the finger, lay on the sheets of metal leaf and press gently into place with a soft lint-free cloth. If the leaf cracks or two sheets don't quite meet, patch it with small pieces of leaf. Let it dry for a day and then dust off all the little tags and shreds.

Tape your paper pattern on the surface to be decorated, but be careful not to paste the tape on the leaf, for the leaf might be pulled off. Now trace the pattern with a sharp pencil. You will not need carbon paper as the lines will show clearly on the gold leaf.

Remove the paper carefully.

With a fine point drawing pen, outline the design in India ink, then, using a small brush, fill in the background with India ink. Work as quickly and smoothly as you can. The first coat of ink will not completely cover the leaf, but *do not go over it once it is dry!* The wet ink will dissolve the dry ink and cause it to lump and crack. Correct any place where you have gone over the line onto the gold leaf by gently lifting the ink with a slightly moist brush.

DESIGNS FOR BLACK AND GILDED BOXES

99

When the ink is dry, spray your work with an even coat of acrylic finish and allow it to dry. This will seal the design so that you may apply a second coat of India ink. Correct any mistakes and again seal it with acrylic.

The two top patterns were originally intended to be used for fretwork, but we have copied them for gold-leaf decorations on small boxes. The hexagonal design, without the frame, is particularly nice on a round box.

A black tin box with a traditional wild rose design in gold leaf.

The Art and Application of Illumination

Illumination is a term applied to the embellishment of written or printed texts with gold and colors, and is an ancient and beautiful art. Illumination may seem to have limited application if you think of it only as a form of decoration used on ancient religious manuscripts like the Book of Kells (a magnificent Irish work of the eighth century). But with a little imagination one can find handsome and unusual applications for this technique. This is not, of course, a Victorian craft, but since Cassell considers it worthy of study we won't quibble over a few centuries.

Throughout the middle ages, when literature was only produced in the form of manuscript, this art was of great importance and was highly developed. But when printing superseded written books illumination languished, and finally became extinct. Since the revival of Gothic architecture, however, this beautiful art has again been brought into notice. In modern times it has more especially been practised by ladies, to whose graceful taste and delicate touch it seems more particularly adapted. Indeed, as an employment for their leisure hours, nothing could be more appropriate, and the great popularity to which it has attained, cannot be a matter of surprise.

The modern art of illumination, like modern Gothic architecture, is entirely governed by mediaeval precedents. We will point out briefly the characteristics of the various periods, and the different methods of treatment adopted, as by this means we shall best enable the student to carry out his own designs with correctness and beauty.

The first great school which prevailed in these islands flourished chiefly in Ireland, and produced many beautiful works. . . . The principal characteristic of this style was its intricate interlaced ribbon ornament. The

initials are much filled with interlaced ribbon ornaments, mostly in black and white (see Figs. 1 and 2). Panels within the letters, and also borders, are filled up with elongated forms of lizards, birds, &c. (see Fig. 3), and any imitation of natural flowers and foliage is avoided.

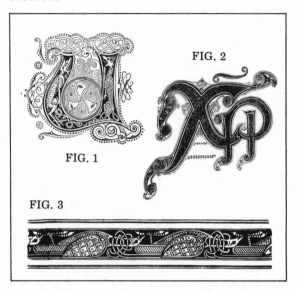

FIG. 2

FIG. 1

FIG. 3

About the time of Charlemagne (early ninth century) the MSS. are distinguished by simple and massive letters, the decorative features of which are derived from classical forms, such as the acanthus. In this the initial letters are plain gold bands, having panels which are frequently filled with interlacing Celtic ornaments; but this like the interlacing work used in other parts of the decoration, is of a bolder and more open treatment than in the previous style. Heads and whole animals are sometimes introduced.

The tenth century Anglo-Saxon illumination is peculiar to this country. In initials the interlaced work is still retained (see Fig. 4), but what is chiefly characteristic of the style is found in the borders which surround the

text. They consist of massive gold bars with geometrical corners and center ornaments, entwined with foliage of a graceful, though severe and conventional character.

In the twelfth century, we find a new style developed, scrollwork of a bold design forms its chief characteristic. . . . We have spiral scrolls, springing frequently from the tails of lizard-like animals and terminating in flowers or leaves. Small portions of the scrolls often turn over and spread at their endings, the reverse side thus shown being of the contrasting or complementary color to the scroll itself (see Fig. 5). The grounds are now frequently of gold, silver, and rich color.

Late in the thirteenth century the coloring became heavy and indistinct. The initials are small, but have elongated extremities, sometimes extending down the whole side of the page. . . . The colors employed are for the most part pink, blue, and green, shaded with their deeper tones, and delicately hatched with white lines. . . . Conventional animal forms appear, and also leaves. This style is shown in Fig. 6.

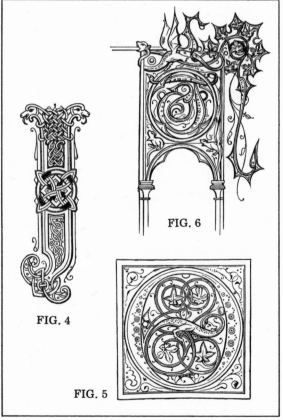

FIG. 6

FIG. 4

FIG. 5

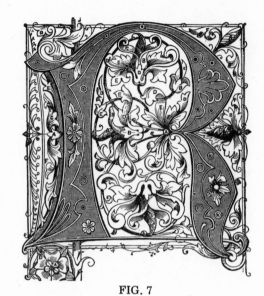

FIG. 7

FOURTEENTH CENTURY COLORS

Ground, *within the Initial,* gold; *without,* green, *excepting the spaces marked F, which are* purple.
Parts of the Initial shaded with vertical lines, scarlet; *with horizontal lines,* blue. *Hair-lines dividing these colors,* white.

A. Yellow, shaded with orange, scarlet, and crimson.
B. Pink, shaded with purple, and lighted with white.
C. Blue, shaded with black and lighted with its own tints or white.
D. Scarlet, shaded with crimson and lighted with orange.
E. Green, shaded with black and lighted with yellow.
F. Purple lighted with pink and white.
Stems, yellow shaded with burnt sienna; outline, black; outer boundary lines, scarlet.

In the fourteenth century, ornament is more lavishly employed on every part. The capital letters are rendered peculiar by consisting of two flat colors fitted into one another, and divided by a white thread line (see Fig. 7). Of these letters the colors generally are red and blue, or gold and blue. Fine line ornaments in color are drawn with a pen round the capitals and borders. Raised gold backgrounds were common in this century.

In the fifteenth century the art is generally considered to have become debased. It is characterised by imitations of flowers, leaves, and animals in their natural colors, very slightly, if at all, conventionalised, and generally on a gold ground (see Fig. 8).

In illumination, purity and brilliancy of color are of the highest value and some attention should be given to a judicious selection of colors. . . . It is only by colors so placed as to produce what are known as harmony, and as contrast, that good results are to be obtained. The effect of harmony on the eye is of a soothing nature, that of contrast of an exciting one. Generally in illumination the latter effect is the one chiefly aimed at.

As a rule, warm tones should be used more sparingly than cold and. . .extremely vivid colors should be used with caution. Among the primary colors blue may be used most freely, red next, and lastly yellow. The secondary colors, with the exception of orange, may be used more lavishly than the primary. Grey, black, white, and metals will be found to relieve any color with which they may be placed in contrast. For this reason colors are almost invariably separated in il-

lumination by outlines of black, or, in some styles, with black and a hair-line of white, or a line of white alone.

In the employment of metal the student will do well to follow the old heraldic rule of keeping "color upon metal, and metal upon color." No illumination looks really well without gold, and where the ground work of initials and other ornaments can be formed by it, it should, so far as the style followed will permit, be employed.

Diapers employed with good effect. . . chiefly as groundwork to fill the panelling of initial letters, and as backgrounds. . . . Some knowledge of diapers will be useful, they are small repetitive designs, usually diamond shaped. We give several illustrations of them. The simplest, and one of the best, would consist of a gold ground indented with lines, and sometimes with dots (Fig.9). Others may be made as in Figs. 10, 11, and 12.

FIG. 8

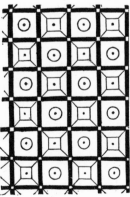

FIG. 9

FIG. 10

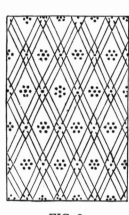

FIG. 11

FIG. 12

Illuminated Backgammon Board

The design for this backgammon board was adapted from a tenth-century border and medallion illustrated in the *Household Guide*. The finished product was so attractive that we added two small rings along one side and, between games, hung it on the wall as a picture. This board and a box for the counters and dice, decorated in the same manner, would make a choice gift for any important gamester in your life.

You will need:

Cold Press, medium-weight illustration board, 22" by 25"
T square, triangle and drawing board are very helpful
Tracing paper
Watercolor brushes, sizes 1 and 2
Paintbrush, 1" wide
Artist's acrylic paints
Artist's oil paint (crimson)
Gold leaf and size
Technical fountain pen with a No. 2 point, or drawing pen
Technical ink or India ink

Razor knife
Plywood, or Masonite, 25" by 22", ½" thick
Decorative molding, 8 feet of ½" wide
Small finishing nails
White glue
Clear acrylic finish
Felt

Cut the illustration board to the correct size with a razor knife. Make sure that it is perfectly straight and that the corners are square.

Mix a quantity of acrylic paint and water, approximately ¼ cup, to the color of old parchment, using yellow ochre, black and burnt sienna. With a 1" brush, paint the entire surface of the illustration board with clear water. While it is still damp, but not puddly, paint it again with the parchment color.

When the board is perfectly dry, block in *very lightly in pencil* the outlines of the borders and playing areas. See Fig. 13. This is where the drawing board, T square, and triangle are very helpful. It is not necessary to indicate the circular medallions.

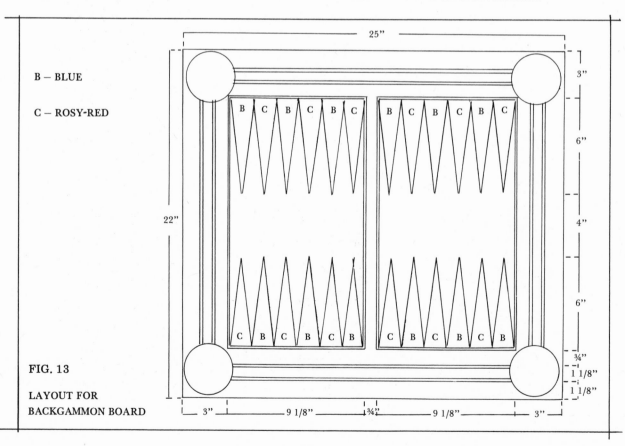

B – BLUE

C – ROSY-RED

FIG. 13

LAYOUT FOR
BACKGAMMON BOARD

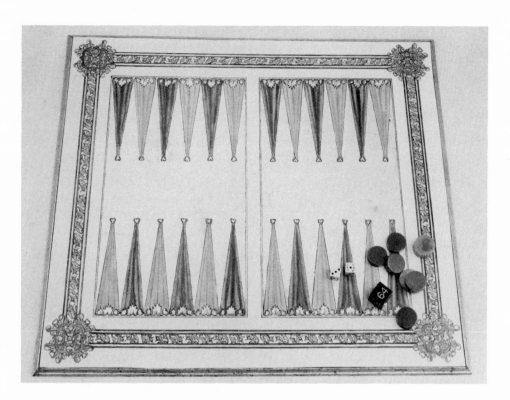

A tenth-century design adapted for an illuminated
backgammon board. The design is done in blue,
rosy-red, and gold on a parchment-colored background.

A – GOLD LEAF
B – BLUE
C – ROSY-RED
D – PARCHMENT

FIG. 14

CORNER DETAIL, BACKGAMMON BOARD
(ACTUAL SIZE)

Tips of all the curled leaves are touched with gold leaf.

Trace the full-scale drawing, Fig. 14, with a soft, black pencil and transfer it on to one corner of the illustration board. You may do this by simply laying the traced drawing face down, positioning it between the guide lines and with a hard pencil, drawing over the lines from the back. Enough carbon will be transferred to the board from the original pencil lines to enable you to see the outlines. Transfer the other corners in the same way. Fill in the rest of the border pattern and points by moving the tracing as necessary.

Pencil in any lines that do not show clearly, and gently, so as not to roughen the surface of the paper, erase any excess guide lines.

Into a small amount of gold size, mix just enough crimson artist's oil paint to color the size a distinct red. Paint the areas to be leafed with an even coat of size. The red coloring will help you to see more easily what you are doing. The areas to be gold are marked with an A on Fig. 14. The playing area and border backgrounds are solid gold and the curled ends of the leaves are brushed with gold. Allow the size to dry until it is just barely sticky when touched, and then start to lay

the leaf upon it, gently tapping it down either with the tips of your fingers or with a wad of soft tissue. Don't be distressed if the leaf tears or cracks; just patch it with small pieces of leaf and pat it into place. Don't try to rub off the loose shreds but let it dry in a warm place for six to ten hours and then brush away the excess with a soft paint brush.

Paint the rest of the board as shown in Fig. 14. The paint plan for the points is given on Fig. 13. We used a paler tint of both the red and blue to paint the first coat and then shaded it with a second coat of a darker color.

Outline the entire design with black ink. A technical fountain pen is invaluable for this operation as it can be used against a straight-edge without so much danger of smearing.

Glue the illustration board to the plywood backing which has been cut to the exact size. Measure and cut the molding to frame the board and cover the raw edges. Glue and nail it into place. Paint or gold leaf the molding as you choose.

Give the board three or four coats of clear acrylic finish. Paste green felt on the back to finish it nicely.

To restore the freshness of grapes, cut the stalk of each bunch and put it into wine, as flowers are set in water.

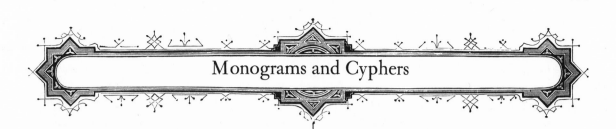

Monograms and Cyphers

Throughout history, the use of cyphers and monograms has been widespread, particularly among artists, craftsmen, and merchants. They were used, as was the crest by the nobility, for identification in ages before the majority of people could read. But such emblems have always been popular, especially so in the mid-nineteenth century when newly affluent groups made a bid for social recognition.

The employment of monograms in various ways is, in our own times, exceedingly fashionable. Upon an envelope, or upon note-paper, a well designed monogram forms a graceful ornament; it implies less ostentation than a crest, and is indeed, according to ancient usage, the proper distinctive symbol of those who are not, according to the laws of heraldry, entitled to use armorial bearings. The monogram of our own day owes its popularity to the renewed appreciation of mediaeval art.

A monogram, as its name implies, consists of the initials or letters of a name combined in some fanciful manner, and properly, in such a way as to form but a single decorative character. The characters used are commonly those which belong to some of the more angular alphabets (as Gothic). The distinctive characteristics of a monogram may be seen in Fig. 1.

The laws to be observed in the construction of these devices are few and simple. In a monogram the first thing to be observed is that it be symmetrical and pleasing to the eye, so far as is consistent with legibility, and the following points should be bourne in mind: The principal letter which is commonly the initial of the surname, should be made most prominent. In most instances this can be done by making it of a larger size. It is allowable sometimes, when found conducive to the harmony and beauty of the work, to take some liberties with the exact forms of the letters, if this can be done without destroying their individual character and significance. Although to some extent a monogram is supposed to be of the nature of an enigma, and, therefore, not necessarily to be read at first glance, the letters should be so arranged that each may on closer inspection be clearly made out.

In our illustration Fig. 2 we have shown an example of monograms embodying the Christian name only, and in which the whole of the letters composing it are introduced. Almost all the shorter female name may be combined into graceful monograms in the same manner, and a device containing the Christian name only is naturally in favor among young ladies, since no change of monogram is then necessary upon change of name in marriage. We have given, in Figs. 3, 4, and 5, what appear to us good typical combinations of the initials of Christian and surnames, which will help the designer.

The cypher consists of the letters merely interlaced, but not combined. In the single cypher, the letters occur once only, and in their usual order, while the double or rever-

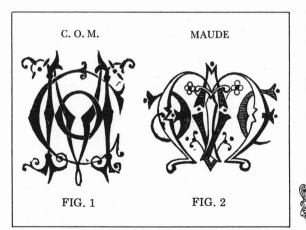

C. O. M.   MAUDE

FIG. 1   FIG. 2

sed cypher is rendered more symmetrical by the letters being repeated in a reversed order. The distinctive characteristics of a double and single cypher are shown in Figs. 6 and 7. Flowing Italian letters are employed, and the great points are; the attainment of graceful curves, and the proper filling of a certain boundary line, either real or imaginary, for, when the cypher is not intended to fill a certain fixed space, it is frequently brought into an oval form, as being the most graceful (see Fig. 6).

Certain interlacings and interweavings in cyphers are always good in effect. In designing the double cypher (see Fig. 7), which is a convenient method of gaining symmetry with letters which will not otherwise readily assume a decorative arrangement, the easier method is first to write the letters, then to copy them on tracing-paper, and turning the latter to retrace them on the reverse side, interweaving the two initials of the surname as much as may be desired. This will readily give a general double effect on the tracing-paper, which may afterwards be worked out ornamentally.

To make your monogram or cypher, trace your initials from one of the sample alphabets and arrange it in a pleasing pattern. (Tracing paper is a great help.) Draw your monogram neatly in India ink, and have your local printer make up a box of informal note paper using it. If the design lends itself to color, paint it with watercolors, or, to be really extravagant, use some of the ideas shown in the preceding entry on illumination.

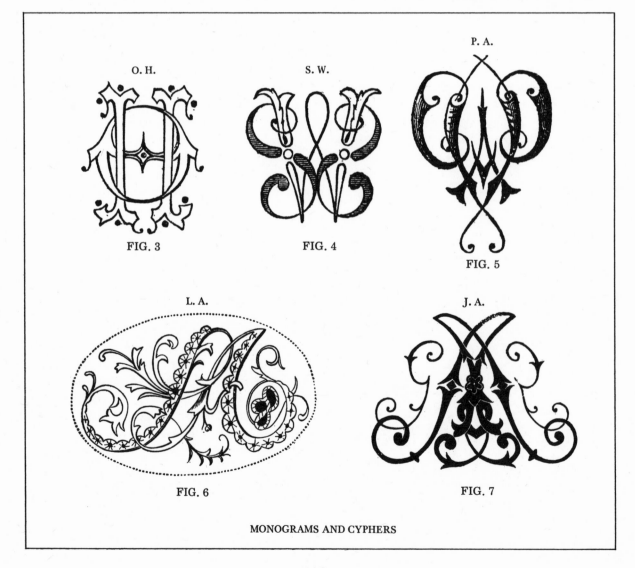

O. H.

FIG. 3

S. W.

FIG. 4

P. A.

FIG. 5

L. A.

FIG. 6

J. A.

FIG. 7

MONOGRAMS AND CYPHERS

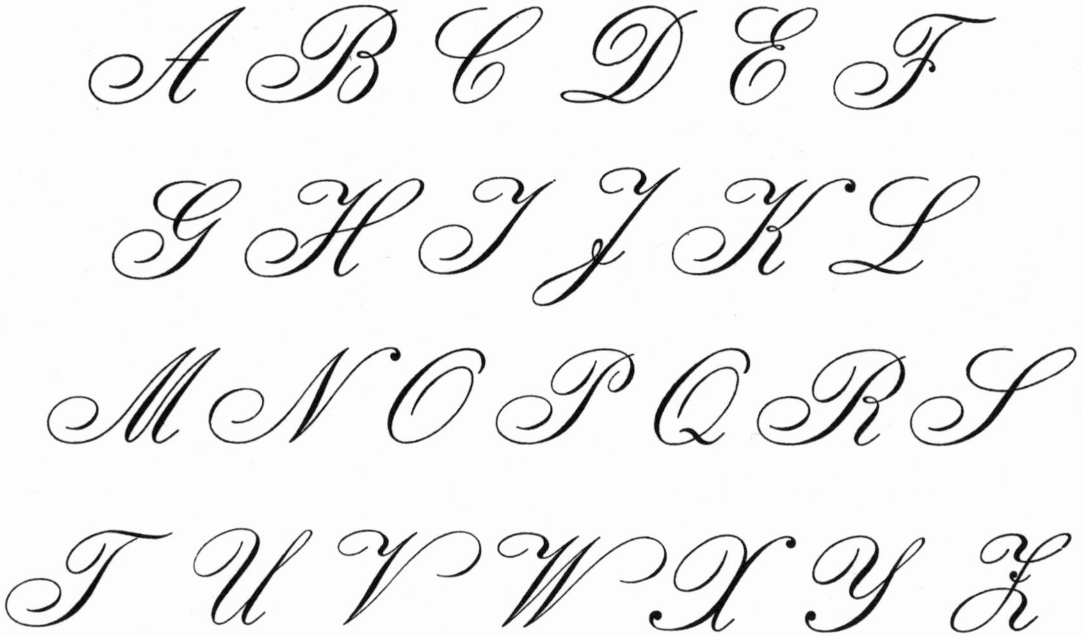

A B C D E F
G H I J K L
M N O P Q R S
T U V W X Y Z

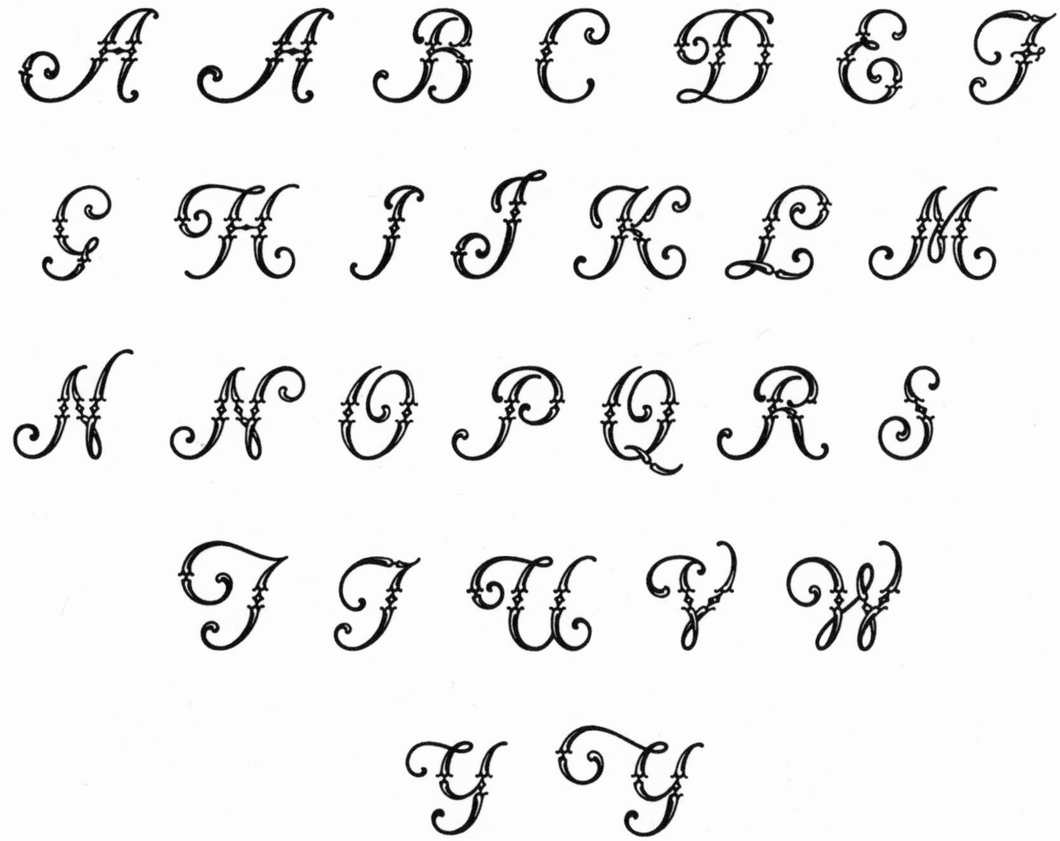

A A B C D E F
G H I J K L M
N N O P Q R S
T T U V W
Y Y

Articles for Gifts and Fancy Fairs

These elegant little tidbits of silk and satin are really most appealing. In London antique shops that specialize in Victoriana and ephemera you occasionally see vintage specimens at astonishing prices. (Even Queen Victoria and ladies of her court made this sort of thing for charity bazaars, where anything made by royal hands was much in demand.) Although not many of us have a pressing need for penwipers or bodkin cases, they might be the perfect gift for the woman "who has everything." Or, you can sew loops of gold cord on them and use them for Christmas ornaments.

Cassell's directions are clear with careful reading, and, who knows? These very same directions may have been followed by Victoria herself!

Turkish Slipper

Materials: a little cardboard, or a couple of old playing cards, some white silk, colored satin or velvet, gold and white seed beads, a bodkin, a thimble, and some white pins. Colored and white sewing silk.

Cut from card two pieces of the shape of Fig. 1. Cover each on one side with white silk.

An easy way to do this is to cut the silk to the same shape as the cardboard, but a good 3/8" larger all around. Clip the margin almost to the cardboard around all of the curves and then sew from one side to another across the back, pulling the fabric tightly over the cardboard. See Fig. 2. Sew the two covered pieces neatly together, back to back, leaving a small space between the stitches at the heel to insert the bodkin.

Cut one piece of very thin card, the shape of Fig. 3. Cover one side with colored satin or velvet [in the same manner as above]. Work on the pattern in gold and crystal seed beads. Cut white silk the same size, tack it on as a lining, turning a little bit in all round; sew it all round. This finished, make the toe of the slipper. Sew the two long sides of the toe that come to a point to the two sides of the toe part of the sole. Fig. 4 shows the appearance of the complete slipper. Put in the bodkin in the way indicated, and stick small pins, such as the haberdashers use for ribbons, all round the edge of the sole and edge of the front of the toe. Fit the thimble into the toe.

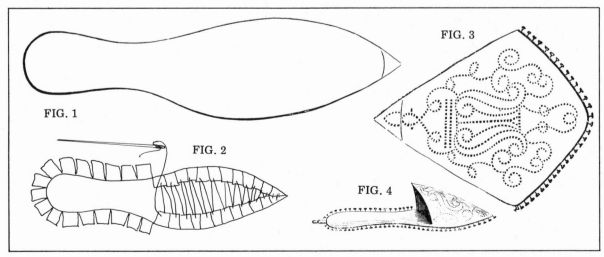

FIG. 1

FIG. 2

FIG. 3

FIG. 4

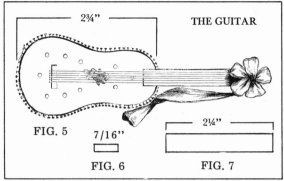

FIG. 5
7/16"
FIG. 6   FIG. 7
THE GUITAR
2¾"
2¼"

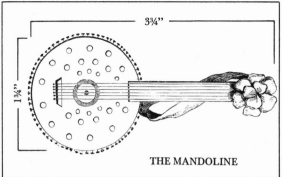

THE MANDOLINE
3¾"
1¾"

Guitar

This is a particularly pretty little article. The materials required are a little piece of light, bright-green satin, a very little bit of gros-grain ribbon; green, black and pale yellow fine sewing silk; and a little narrow, white sarcenet ribbon; a few gold and red spangles, some small white pins, and a gold lion of embossed paper; also some thin card [cardboard] and a little gum.

From the card, cut two pieces like the body of the guitar. Cover these with the green satin, by tacking it one end to the other, across the wrong side [as you did for the slipper]. Cut a little piece of card, like Fig. 6. Cover it very neatly with black, and stitch it to one piece of the body, as the bridge shown in Fig. 5. It must be stitched upright, on end. Cut two pieces of card, like Fig. 7; cover each with black silk, stitch one to the upper piece of the body of the guitar, with invisible stitches. Then with the yellow silk imitate the strings, beginning just beyond the bridge, carrying them over the bridge, up to the top of the back piece. Before putting on the strings, fix the lion in the center, and the red and gold spangles round it with thick gum. Neatly stitch the second black piece to the other part of the guitar body. Then sew the two black pieces neatly together with black silk, uniting the tops, and with green silk sew the two pieces of the guitar together. Make a loop of white sarcenet ribbon at the top of the black part, and cover the join with a handsome knot of white bows. To complete it, stick small white pins around the body of the guitar at the edges, between the stitches of the sewing.

Mandoline

For the latter instrument the round may be made smaller. The materials are a little bit of white satin, a little bit of red, some black gros-grain, some narrow red satin ribbon, a pennyworth of spangles, white and black and yellow sewing silk, and some small white pins; also a little cardboard and gum.

Cut two rounds as shown in the illustration, and two straight pieces as shown for the neck. Cover both of the latter on one side with black gros-grain. Cover the round, one with white, the other with cherry-colored satin, each on one side only. Cut a bridge for the mandoline; cover it with black, and stitch it on. Paint a circle on the white satin to form the hole in the center, or make it of spangles. Gilt circles can be bought in paper as well as gilt lions. Gum the spangles round the circles. Stitch one one of the black pieces for the neck and then form the strings of the yellow silk. Stitch the other black piece to the red circle. Stitch both black pieces together, and then the circles together with white silk. Stick pins all round the circle only, and make a loop of cherry ribbon, and a handsome knot of bows at the top.

Fish Pincushion

Materials: a small card, a little bit of grey silk, a little bit of Brussels net, a few pins, and a bit of wadding.

Cut two cards, the shape as shown; cover each on one side with grey silk, tacked across the back from edge to edge, every way straining it tight. Color on one side with India ink; draw the eyes, rings round them, the nos-

trils, and the division of the head. Cover both pieces with white net. Sew the two together; when side is sewn, put a little wadding between. When nearly sewn all round, stuff in with the scissors more wadding, if wanted. There should be enough to make the fish look as plump as a real one. If a little powder scent is put in with the wadding it is an improvement. Put on the fins and tail with pins in the manner shown, and between them, all round the fish, place pins close in.

Hand Penwiper

Materials: a piece of new white card, stout, such as Bristol board, a little piece of black velvet and any fancy material; a little white blond lace, passementerie, chalk seed beads, and black sewing silk.

Cut the hand out of the white card. Dot on the glove seams with pen and ink. The card is cut a little longer than what is shown in the illustration, to allow the penwiper to be attached. Cut the shape of the cuff in two pieces, either both of black velvet, or one of

velvet and one of fancy material for the wrong side. Work on the motto, "No hands should be idle," to the black velvet with chalk beads. On the wrong side stitch the two cuff pieces together, and turn them. Before attaching them to the hand, cut four pieces out of fancy material, a little smaller, and notch the edges. Sew these first to the hand, and the ornamental piece over them. Then run on two pieces of blond lace, one each way at the wrist of the hand, in the way shown, and between them place a row of passementerie.

Bellows

Materials: card, some silk or satin, some spangles, a bodkin, pins, and sewing silk.

Cut two pieces of card, the shape as shown; cover each on one side with silk or satin; sew them together. Leave open a space for the bodkin, which forms the nose. On the right side fix spangles with gum, a circle in the center, and the rest dotted about. All round the edge, between the sewing, place pins.

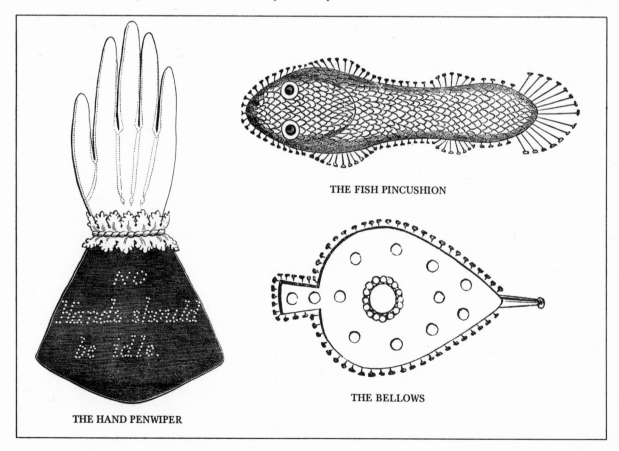

THE FISH PINCUSHION

THE BELLOWS

THE HAND PENWIPER

Work-Box Furniture

The daughters in a well-ordered Victorian houshold spent long hours doing plain sewing. It was the visiting seamstress who did the complicated fitting and sewing required for their elaborate toilettes of the period. One trusts that the miniature furniture described here — disguising pins, needles, and bodkins — helped to ease the boredom of that dull chore.

By following the directions given below, some very pretty sets of miniature furniture may be made, every article of which is of some use in connection with the work-box.

Pole Screens

A sheet of Bristol board is necessary to make these ornaments, and either some skill in drawing flowers is required, or a few of the German raised scraps and wreaths used for Valentines may be purchased.

Cut four squares of the cardboard and take off the corners; they must all be exactly alike, and according to Fig. 1. Put a well finished group of flowers on two of them. A

little plain bright gold paper is needed. Rule a narrow strip off the paper and then cut it carefully. Gum the gold paper and bind the edges of all four cards. Gum some turquoise ribbon from A to B of Fig. 1, of course on the wrong side, and join it to one of the plain cards of the same shape, so as to make a needle-book.

The other two cards are similarly united. Next fit each with a flannel or cashmere needle-book, stocked with needles.

Next cut four cards the shape of Fig. 2; upon two of them put wreaths of flowers, and bind the edges with gold paper.

Cut four more cards a little smaller, bind these with blue ribbon, and then sew them together with a narrow ribbon to make a pincushion. Fill the pincushion, but not so full as to prevent the card from setting quite flat. Gum the other cards on, one each side. Take a short knitting-needle, make a hole through the entire pincushion, and put it through; fix it with sealing wax on the wrong side. Twist some blue ribbon round the needle, fixing the ends with gum. Fix the needle-book and

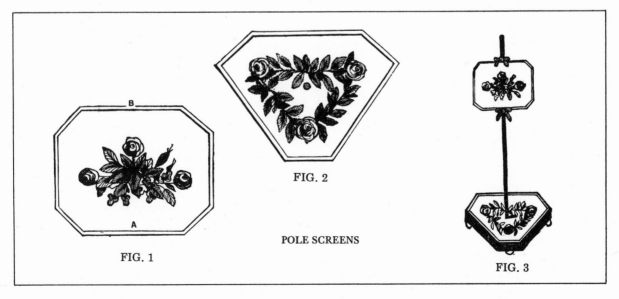

FIG. 2

FIG. 1

POLE SCREENS

FIG. 3

knitting-needle by the plain side, leaving the painted one to open. Fix with sealing-wax three China shirt-buttons as feet. Fig. 3 shows the appearance of the screen finished.

Chair

To make the first chair, cut out a card the shape of Fig. 4, score along the broken lines A to A on the outside. Cover both sides with satin, first cutting a slit at B. Leave a space in the sewing at the edge at C, only just large enough to admit a bodkin, which may be seen there. Now bend the card round, so as to form a base for the lower part of the chair and sew it together; bend the places where they turn to keep a good square. Cut two squares like Fig. 5, cover one side with satin; sew it in to form the bottom. Make the other with a pincushion at the top.

Before putting this on cut two pieces of 3/8" dowel, one ½" long the other ¾" long. Whittle down one end of each until the whit-

tled ends fit snugly into the holes of a spool. Make a hole through the fabric and cardboard on each side of the base of the chair, just large enough so the unwhittled end of the dowels fit easily. Tack one end of a cloth tape measure to the spool, and fit the spool inside the base of the chair, securing it in place with the two bits of dowel run through the holes in the base of the chair. Put the free end of the tape measure through the slit in the front of the chair and sew a button on the tape measure so it will not slip back through the slit. Rewind the tape on the spool by turning the dowels, which may be finished on the outside with wooden beads glued on. Sew the seat of the chair into place.

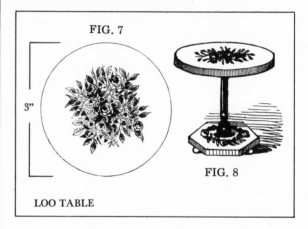

FIG. 7 — FIG. 8 — LOO TABLE

Loo Table

Loo was a popular cardgame of the period, somewhat on the order of poker. One suspects that Victorian ladies were as addicted to gambling as were their grandmothers in the Regency period.

Cut two circles of cardboard like Fig. 7. Draw a group of flowers on one, and bind them both with gold paper. Make them up into a needle-book for large sized darning, tapestry, or small crochet needles. Cut a stand for the table like Fig. 2, of the polescreen, and make it up the same way, with feet and pincushion. A bodkin makes the stem of the table. Make a tube of cardboard, a little longer than the bodkin [we used a plastic drinking straw], to make the pedestal of the table which is a bodkin case. Fig. 8 represents the table complete.

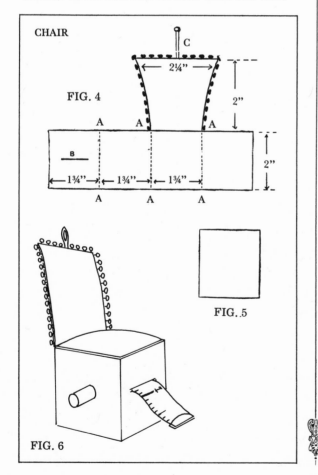

CHAIR — FIG. 4 — 2¼" — C — A A A — 2" — B — 1¾" 1¾" 1¾" — A A A — 2" — FIG. 5 — FIG. 6

Fans

It is a pity that this feminine accessory has been relegated to the ball park and burlesque stage. Earlier centuries had an elaborate code of fan movements, usually of amorous import. Fans were a necessary adjunct to courtship and flirtation — to conceal a maiden's blush (or lack of one), to chastise a forward beau with a tip on the wrist and a "La, Sir!," or to open with a snap as a sign of pique. The Victorian taste for the romantic and antique brought a renewed interest in the art of fan making and a major exhibition was held at the South Kensington Museum in London in 1870.

The traditional folding fan is difficult to make and requires special tools and skills, but Cassell describes two types of fans that are easier to reproduce: a Feather Fan and a Bouquet Fan.

Feather Fan

A beautiful feather fan, which cannot be folded, may be made in the following manner;

— A segment of a circle, cut out in cardboard, should be taken and feathers, such as the tail feathers of the peacock, cut to the required length, and placed with their quill ends towards the angle, the other ends radiating outwards as they do in the spread tail of the living bird. These are secured in their places with a needle and thread, and by glue. Another and shorter row is then placed upon them, so as to conceal the quills, and secured as before; and afterwards similar rows using smaller feathers. When the feathers have thus been brought down to the angle of the cardboard, that part will have to be inserted in a handle split to receive it. The back of the cardboard may be covered with silk or gold paper.

The color and decorations of this fan may be done as your fancy dictates, or you might follow the design of a very famous fan given to Queen Elizabeth the First by Sir Francis Drake.

Queen Elizabeth had a Ffan of ffeathers white and redd, the handle of gold, enameled with a half-moone of mother-of perles, within

THE SOUTH KENSINGTON
PRIZE FAN MOUNT

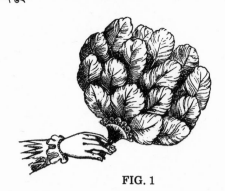

FIG. 1

that a half-moone of sparks of dyamonds, and a few seed perles on the one side, having her majestie's picture within it, and on the backsyde thereof a device with a crowne over it. Fig. 1 is an illustration of a fan belonging to that sovereign.

An elegant fan, be it of feathers or of silk with a finely painted landscape, has been used, essentially, as a fashion accessory — although, we are told that "the severe English matron of the fourteenth century carried a feather fan with a handle a yard long, with which she was accustomed to administer personal chastisement to her children and servants."

Cheap fans were intended primarily to stir up a refreshing breeze, but Cassell describes another use for them.

The Spaniards sell cheap fans at the doors of the amphitheater where the bullfights take place, everybody buys them. When the questionable amusement of the day is over and twilight comes on, the more innocent sport of destroying these fans begins, and a temporary illumination is got up by each spectator setting fire to his fan.

Bouquet Fan

Cassell describes the Bouquet Fan as "cheap, but elegant" and it is not very difficult to make. However we haven't thought of a practical application for it other than to set on fire at the conclusion of a bullfight.

You will need:

Strong, lightweight paper, 28" long by 4½" wide (use parchment if you can find it at your art store)
Two pieces of 1/16" thick wood, 3/8" wide by 9" long
A piece of lightweight cardboard, ½" by 2¼"
India ink and lettering pen
2" length of light wire
White glue
10" of cord
Three silk tassels
Tracing paper
Utility razor knife
Vise
Sandpaper
Small drill

Cut a 26" by 4½" strip of parchment for the mount and mark it off with very light pencil lines into ½" segments. Now sketch in your decorations. These fans are not suitable for landscapes, but should be decorated with borders or with radiating star patterns. We gold leafed one side and decorated the other with a black scroll design above a wide gold band. We scalloped the outside edge and bordered it with black and gold bands. See Fig. 2. Instructions for gold leafing appear in Black and Gilded Box (see page 99).

When the ink and leaf are dry, fold the fan along the pencil lines, making the creases

FIG. 2

A portion of the mount.

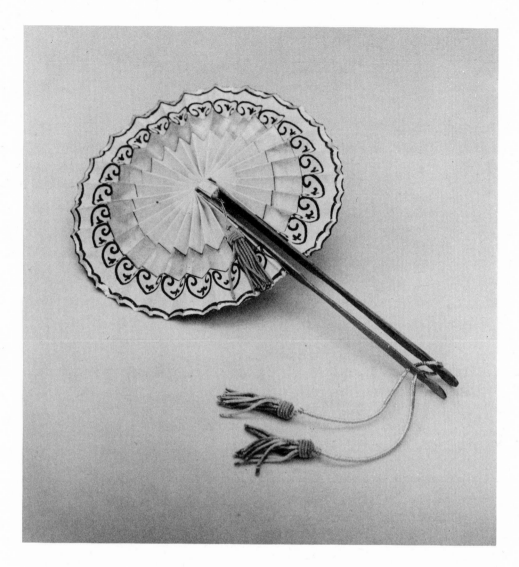

A tasseled, parchment fan with a border design in
black and gold.

as sharp and accurate as possible. Open the fan and erase the pencil marks. Make a hole with a darning needle through all the folds of the fan about ¼" from the bottom and wire them tightly together leaving a small loop of wire at the bottom. Wrap a ½" strip of lightweight cardboard around the end to conceal the wire and glue the cardboard in place. Sew a tassel on to the wire loop. See Fig. 3.

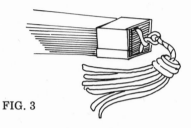

FIG. 3

Trace the pattern given in Fig. 4 and transfer it to one of the sticks. Clamp both sticks firmly together in a vise and with a razor knife, carefully cut away the excess wood around the pattern. Shape one side at a time being careful to keep both sides the same. Sand the edges well while the sticks are still in the vise. Remove them and drill two holes (as shown in Fig. 4) in one stick. Give the sticks a coat of varnish or paint as desired.

When the sticks are dry, glue them one each to the first fold on either end of the mount. End A of the sticks should be 1/8" above the binding of the mount.

Thread a cord through the holes in the stick as shown in Fig. 5. This is to hold the fan open and/or closed. Sew tassels on each end.

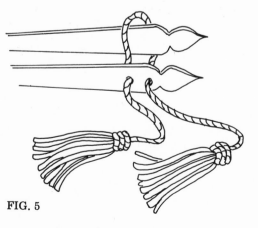

FIG. 5

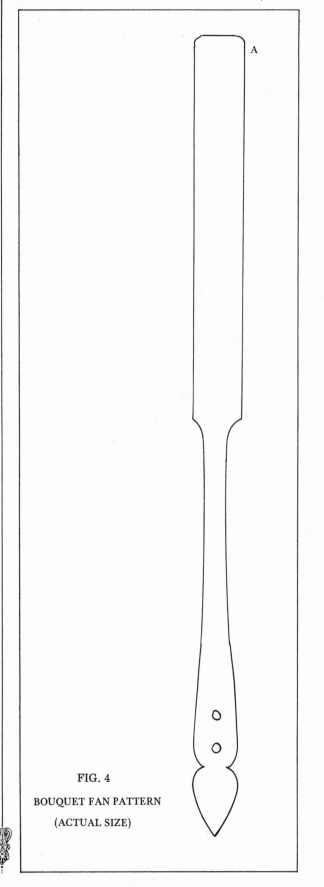

FIG. 4

BOUQUET FAN PATTERN

(ACTUAL SIZE)

Paper Flower Making

Cassell's directions for making these flowers are very detailed and include the suggestion that actual flowers be taken apart, petal by petal, to use as patterns for cutting — a real education in botany for the lady who took him seriously. This approach can produce remarkable results. Mary Delany, a late eighteenth-century artist and student of Hogarth, turned in her seventies to making flower pictures of paper, using much the same technique, and with such accuracy that a noted naturalist of the day said he would not hesitate to use them as models.

The art of paper flower making is an elegant one, and capable of very high perfection. It has also this merit, that, unlike many accomplishments, the very earliest attempts of amateurs are at least pretty, even if unfit to decorate the drawing-room.

It must not be forgotten that the object of the paper flower maker is to imitate nature as closely as possible; therefore the learner should observe flowers well. Whenever it is possible, obtain a fine specimen of whatever flower you desire to copy from the garden or conservatory. Examine it well, and then pick it to pieces. Cut out in white paper models of every size of petal which it bears. Mark on every sized petal as you take the pattern how many of that size the flower contains. Then cut them out in paper of corresponding color, and make them up, as closely imitating the real flower as you possibly can.

At first it will be well to make up a few flowers from the outline patterns we shall give. If these are practiced through the winter months, the learner will be able by the summer to copy from nature, and keep by her her own patterns taken from her own garden.

To make paper flowers a few tools will be needed: a darning egg, various rounded handles of kitchen utensils or hair brushes, a fine pair of scissors, with long points; some glue; some very fine wire, and some strong wire for stems. A large, soft pincushion, is also necessary.

Cabbage Rose

To make a cabbage rose, three sheets of three different shades of deep pink tissue paper are needed, and one of green; also a very little cotton wool, and a reel of green sewing silk. There are five different sized petals used for a cabbage-rose, and a square piece. Take a little piece of wool, and covering it with the square of paper, make it into a little ball the size of a pea, and tie it round as in Fig. 1. You will need two more of these. Then begin to cut out petals. Fold the paper so as to cut eight each time. If the paper is folded too thick it can never be cut well, but on the contrary the scissors are spoiled. Out of the darkest shade cut Figs. 2 and 3, nine of each, and nine of Fig. 4 in the middle shade. These petals are to be crimped.

Crimping is done by rolling the petals, starting at the bottom, one at a time on a pencil. While still on the pencil, push the sides of the rolled petal together toward the centers, pinching the paper so as to make the irregular crisp-looking creases noticed in the heart of a rose. The marks must be very strong, and the leaves quite crimped. Unroll the petal, which should look like Fig. 5.

Stick together with cement by their narrow ends three petals of Fig. 2, three of Fig. 3, and three of Fig. 4, as shown in Fig. 6. Make two more groups in the same way, which will use up all the petals you have.

Cut out in the middle shade of paper nine petals like Fig. 7. Lay each separately on

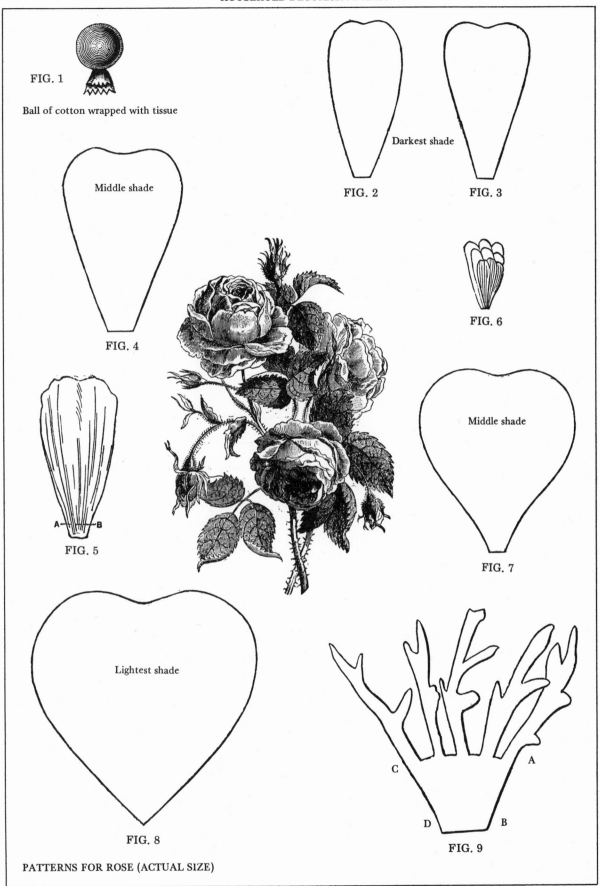

FIG. 1

Ball of cotton wrapped with tissue

Middle shade

Darkest shade

FIG. 2   FIG. 3

FIG. 4

FIG. 6

A——B

FIG. 5

Middle shade

FIG. 7

Lightest shade

C   A

D   B

FIG. 8   FIG. 9

PATTERNS FOR ROSE (ACTUAL SIZE)

the cushion, and with the rounded handle of a darning egg rub it gently, pressing it in the middle till it curls all round. . . . Turn back the extreme edges very slightly with your fingers. Glue three of these petals on the outside of each of the three groups of petals. Then with the cement, fix one of each of the three groups of petals upon one of the three balls shown full size in Fig. 1. Cut off next three more petals of Fig. 2, three of Fig. 3, three of Fig. 4, and crimp them as you did the first. Cement these together in three groups of one each. Then tie the three little balls shown full size in Fig. 1. Cut out next three more petals of Fig. 2, three of Fig. 3, long. Be sure it is tied on very tightly. If the top of the wire has a tiny loop made, it will be more secure. Tie the balls so that the groups of petals attached form a close and well-shaped heart for the rose. The balls must be entirely hidden by the petals. Then in the three spaces between these three groups cement the three little groups of three petals which you have just crimped. Next cut out twenty-four petals like Fig. 8 in the lightest shade. Curl them on the cushion, using the large end of the darning egg. Curl them all back at the edges. Hold the rose in your hand downwards, and put on, by touching the lower point of each leaf with cement. . . the twenty-four Fig. 8 petals, laying them regularly all round, one a little over the other. Now leave the rose to dry, having cemented the base well.

The calyx must be added as soon as the rose is dry. Cut from a sheet of bright pale-green paper, not tissue, a calyx like Fig. 9, keeping the spikes as sharp and natural as possible. It must be united by fastening the side A B to C D by the little bit seen projecting from A to B. Let this dry. Then thoroughly cement the inside, put in a very little wool, enough to fill the cup of the calyx, and slip it up the wire with the part from A to C meeting the swell of the petals to which the cement is attached. If the petals drop too much, the spikes of the calyx may be fastened to them with a touch of cement to support them.

Cut a long strip of green tissue-paper, half an inch wide, and very even. Gum it slightly from A to B and attach this to the calyx. Hold the stem in one hand and roll the paper tightly and smoothly all down the stalk [or use florist's tape]. Leave the flower upside down, to dry completely. The next day, turn the rose petals and curl them any way you like, to imitate nature as closely as possible.

Leaves are never made in paper. They must be bought. Vary them in color as much as possible.

These roses may be made in any shade of pink, from a pale tint to a deep rose color. Yellow roses can also be formed from the same pattern, but are better cut a mere shade smaller in every petal. For a damask rose cut the patterns visibly smaller.

Half-Blown Rosebud

Half-blown buds are very effective. Make them in white paper, slightly tipped with pale pink, or in pink or rose paper, or in orange paper streaked with red, cutting the outsides of the darkest shades, and the darkest towards the stalk. To make one of these deep yellow buds, cut four petals of Fig. 7, in the palest tint. Curl them inwards. Close two over a bud center and two more over that. Then cut eleven of Fig. 8, a still darker shade and eleven more of the darkest of all. Curl and pull them outwards, and let the darker shade be the outer one. To make a bud center, take a piece of cotton wool, tie it to a stalk and cover it with paper as in Fig. 10.

FIG. 10

Stamens and Pistils

Our next instructions will be how to make the hearts, as they are commonly called, but which are known botanically as stamens and pistils. Very fine wire is used for the main stem of the stamen, otherwise when it comes to be added to the flower-stalk, the result

would be too bulky. Exceedingly fine wire can be used for the stamens, dip them in white paint and when dry dip the tips into thick yellow paint to form knobs at the ends. Form the pistil by putting a little cotton wool on the end of the stem by means of cement, shaping it properly and dipping it again into the cement. Paint it emerald green.

Carnation

The carnation is a beautiful flower and easy to make. Cut it in white paper like Fig. 11, and with carmine color a brilliant red band with streaky edges. When quite dry... crimp every petal from A to B.... Six of these circles are used for every flower. It is easiest to cut them out plain first and vandyke the edges, and cut the irregular marks that characterise the flower afterwards. To make them up, cement each all around the center to where the petals divide. Crumple the first one quite close up all around the heart, hiding it entirely, and squeezing the paper as much as possible. Make the next one close, and each future one looser and looser. Finish with the calyx.

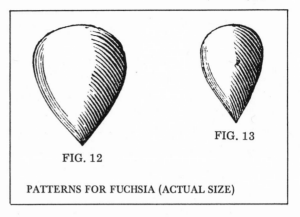

PATTERNS FOR FUCHSIA (ACTUAL SIZE)

FIG. 12

FIG. 13

Fuchsia

The fuchsia must be made of thick paper, or tissue double. Cut four pieces like Fig. 12 of white paper. Mould very slightly with a darning egg handle, and place them round the stamens. Two long wires tipped with yellow ochre make a good center. Close the four petals of the corolla round one another. In scarlet paper, cut four like Fig. 13. Curl them as a fuchsia is moulded. Cement all the narrow parts and place them over the corolla. A purple center may be used with red outer petals, or a scarlet center and long white petals.

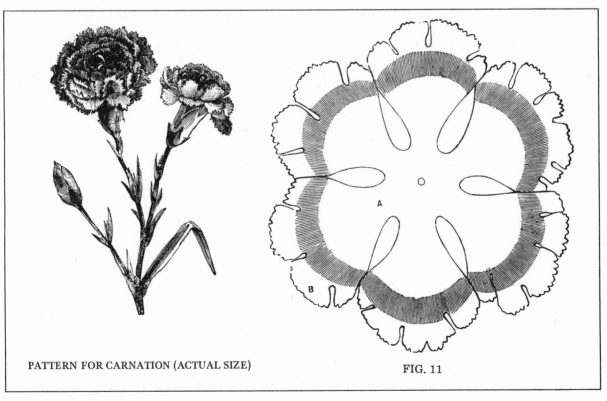

PATTERN FOR CARNATION (ACTUAL SIZE)

FIG. 11

Daisies

Fig. 14 may be used to cut plain or Michaelmas daisies. Daisy hearts can be made with tufts of yellow wool. Fig. 15 represents the daisy calyx.

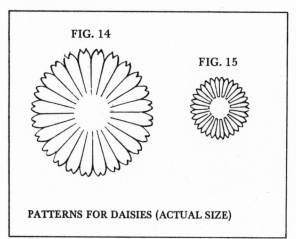

FIG. 14

FIG. 15

PATTERNS FOR DAISIES (ACTUAL SIZE)

Poppy

The poppy needs no diagram. Gather one, and at once whilst it is fresh, pick off its fine petals, lay them flat between a couple of sheets of blotting-paper, and press for twenty-four hours. Then lay the petals on paper and trace the outline of one (choose the best) and cut it out. Cut the pattern larger than the original to allow for crimping. The hearts of poppies are made of black feathers, tied together in a little bunch and cut off flat at the top. Cut five poppy petals of scarlet paper, lay them on the cushion and crimp them well. Attach them around the heart and mount it on a stalk. Gather corn or barley and make a bouquet with the poppies. These poppies are most quickly made and with the corn (wheat) fill vases very prettily, and last all year round.

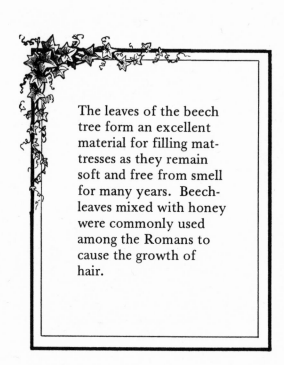

The leaves of the beech tree form an excellent material for filling mattresses as they remain soft and free from smell for many years. Beech-leaves mixed with honey were commonly used among the Romans to cause the growth of hair.

Summer Dressings for Fireplaces

Imagine yourself in a middle-class Victorian parlor on the first day of summer, in 1865. The thermometer stands at fifty-five degrees; you can almost see your breath. But the English are a hardy race and it's officially summer. The maid of all work breathes a sigh of relief; no more parlor fires to make up until fall. The young ladies of the house are busy snipping paper and shredding tarlatan and wasting no time in the rush to cover that last unembellished two square feet, that last bastion of utility, the fireplace.

Simple Fire Paper

Get a sheet of white paper and cut it oval by rounding off the corners. Take a sheet of green tissue paper already doubled, fold it in half lengthwise, and in half across width-way. Fold this once more in half, the lengthway. Then cut it in narrow strips, not quite to the

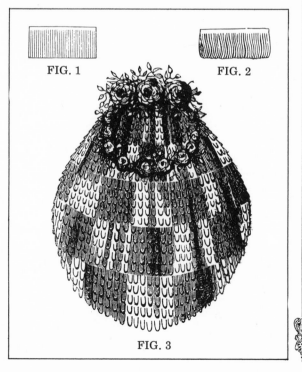

FIG. 1   FIG. 2

FIG. 3

top of the fold, in the manner shown by Fig. 1. There will be eight of these pieces in the sheet. Cut them separately. A fold will be observed in the center of the strips of every piece. Reverse each separately, so that the strips stand out like loops in the cut part, and bring the uncut margins together, Fig. 2.

Tack four green ones, side by side, to the lowest extremity of the oval of paper. Fold a sheet of white tissue paper, and cut it in the same way. Then sew four white pieces by the side of the four green; and, again, next to those, four white, till the width of the paper is covered. Continue cutting more sheets of tissue as they are required. Commence a second row of the cut papers, by reversing the colors, placing four white over the four green, and four green over the four white. Spread the papers farther apart towards the bow of the oval foundation, and press them closer at the ends.

The pieces of tissue paper are fastened to the cartridge foundation by tacking them on with a needle and thread. Sew a few horizontally round the bottom. Fig. 3 shows the shape of the foundation of paper, which is somewhat of an oval.

Green is the best color for brightening up a room; two shades of green, instead of green and white, are the most durable. However the color of the furniture must be considered in choosing the color of the fire paper. Decorate the fire paper with garlands of paper flowers in a suitable color.

Shredded Tarlatan with Myrtle Wreath

For handsome steel grates fire papers are not generally used. Purchase a yard and a half of tarlatan, and pull it entirely to pieces, thread by thread. Fill the grate and fender entirely, as full and lightly as possible. The fire-irons are removed, greased with mutton fat, rolled in paper, and put away in a dry closet for the season. Arrange a slight wreath of myrtle on the top of the heap, or carelessly throw a few well-made muslin roses about the tarlatan in the manner shown in Fig. 4. It is very tasteful to use pale-colored tarlatan, the shade of the furniture, for this purpose, but the tint should be extremely light. A little gold, sold for the purpose, looks well on the colored cloud thus arranged in the stove. Nothing can be prettier than the palest shade of pink tarlatan, unravelled, in the grate, with a few moss roses carelessly arranged about it, and the lace window curtains lined with pink tarlatan throughout, a couple of shades deeper in tone. Very pale green contrasts better with gold than with flowers.

Another elegant way of fitting up a handsome stove for the summer is to order a piece of looking-glass in a plain gilt frame, to fit in as a chimney board. Displace the steel fender, and use a rustic one, with a green tin inside, charged with flower-pots containing plants in bloom. In place of the mantel-shelf valance of fringe, hang point-lace in deep vandykes mounted on silk, edged with a narrow silk fringe, the color of the furniture. Cur-

FIG. 4

FIG. 5

tains of fine lace, lined with colored tarlatan or this silk, may be looped each side with a good effect in some apartments. Fig. 5 shows the disposition of these adornments.

Rustic Fender

We have always liked a fireplace cleaned, freshly blackened with a mixture of powdered lamp-black and vinegar and dressed with a white paper fan for summer and were delighted to find Cassell's "simple and elegant" alternatives. We resisted the fire paper, the unravelled tarlatan, and the lace vandykes, mirror, and draperies, but fell for another of his suggestions — the rustic fender. Ours is shiny white and when backed with a green forest of ferns, adds a cool, fresh touch to the parlor even on the hottest days.

You will need:

Apple branches or other prunings
Gloss white enamel spray paint
Wood filler
Razor knife
Finishing nails

Measure your fireplace opening to determine the length of your fender. The fender should be wider than the opening by several inches. Mark the length and center point on your worktable.

Cut two branches with similar curves about 1½" in diameter and 6" to 9" long. These branches will serve as the vertical end supports (see A, Fig. 6). Next cut two matched branches for the bottom rungs, long enough to overlap the end supports and to cross in the center, as in B, Fig. 6.

The charm of the rustic design is in the natural forms of the wood. However, if the corresponding pieces are too different in general shape, the fender will look unbalanced and sloppy.

Where the branches cross, notch each one with a razor knife so that it fits snugly (Fig. 7) and nail in place with finishing nails.

Countersink the nails and fill the holes with plastic wood.

Proceed by adding the top rungs, C, and fancy trim pieces, D, notching, nailing, and filling as you go. When the entire face is completed add the right angle returns (see E, Fig. 6), they should project approximately 6" to 8".

Spray with several coats of glossy white enamel.

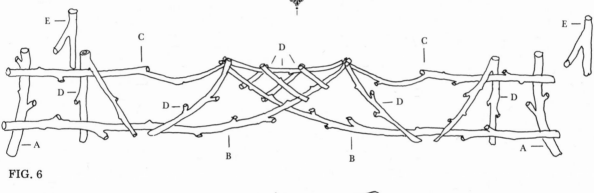

FIG. 6

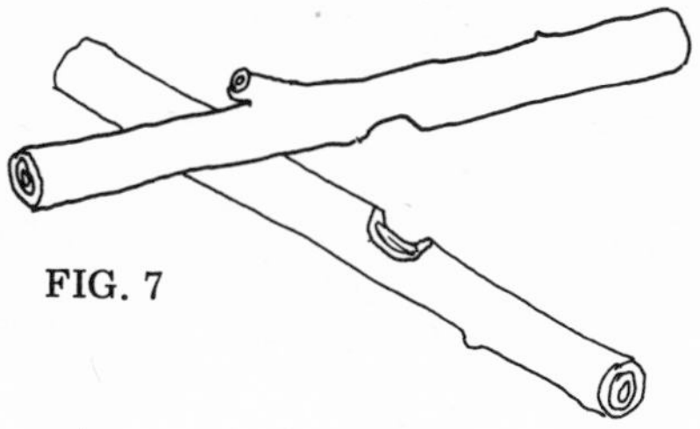

FIG. 7

131

Ornamental Spills

Spills are thin rolls of paper to be lighted in a fire and used as a match, a practical item in a day when friction matches were evil-smelling things. But in keeping with the times, Victorian spills also were embellished with frivolous curly tops and became less useful. If Papa had tried to use one to light his cigar, he most probably would have set his beard on fire.

To make ornamental spills, bright colored papers, and also gold and silver paper are needed. The thick paper is used, and it is best of the same color on both sides. Take gold, silver, blue, scarlet, and rich green to fill one vase, violet, mauve, crimson, yellow, light green, gold and silver for another. Cut a strip of paper an inch wide, and the length of the sheet. Cut a piece off the top as in Fig. 1, and roll it between the fingers into a spiral stem, pointed at the top, and a little broader at the base where the end is pinched, and sewn down neatly so as not to show, see Fig. 2. Then take a strip of the whole length of the paper, and two inches wide. Three inches wide makes the top still handsomer. Cut it in narrow strips to within a quarter of an inch of the top, like Fig. 3, making them very regular and even. The actual roll is to be like Fig. 4. Then curl these strips by twisting each separately and closely round a knitting pin, not letting one twist overlap the other, but exactly meet. It is wrapped tightly the whole length of the strip, and pressed on the needle by the fingers, the needle is then slipped out. Fold the top A to A, in Fig. 3, backwards and forwards in little pleats and sew it to the broad top of the spill. If the curls are not enough to hang all around the spill, add another bunch for the center ones. The spills that surround this need curls on one side only. A pretty variation can be made by cutting strips of gold paper the width of the curls, and gumming them spirally around the stems.

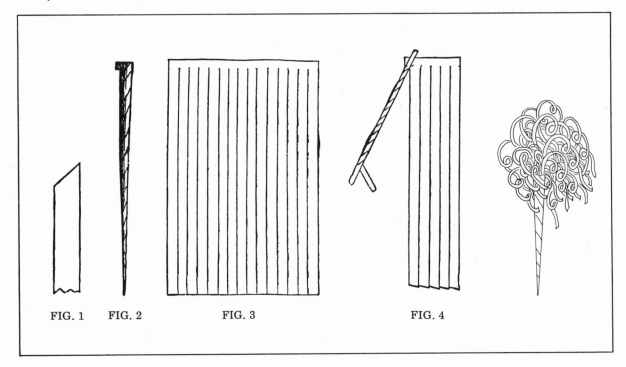

FIG. 1   FIG. 2   FIG. 3   FIG. 4

Fish-Scale Embroidery

Cassell has an endearing quality of being much concerned with household economy — "avoiding unnecessary expenditures" — and he suggests novel uses for found materials: sea-shells, acorns and cones, branches and leaves, and, the oddest of all, fish-scales, for which he suggests an "exquisitely graceful embroidery." (If you can't find — or can't face — the real thing, try iridescent sequins.)

The production of beautiful objects of decoration by no means necessarily involves great outlay and expensive materials. A knowledge of how to utilise trifles which would otherwise be valueless, will often enable the housewife to render her home attractive without expending that money which may be required for other purposes. We are about to show how a species of exquisitely graceful embroidery may be produced, in which the chief material employed is nothing more than the scales of a common fresh water fish.

Fish-scales, sewn upon silk or satin, may be arranged so as to form flowers, leaves, ornamental borders, and also birds, to enrich many of those small articles of taste, which always conduce to throw an air of refinement over a home, and give the visitor a favorable opinion of the occupants. The effect produced by employing a material generally so little regarded as the scales of fishes, is one which will much surprise and gratify those of our readers who have never seen it used in this manner.

The scales of various fishes may be used, but those of the perch are to be preferred, on account of their beautiful serrations. When taken from the fish they should first be thoroughly cleaned, and before they become dry and hard, two holes should be pierced through each, near the roots of the scales.

The best ground is one of pink or blue satin. The pattern should first be drawn to

the required size and traced on the satin using dress-maker's tracing paper. We will suppose that a rose or some similar flower has to be worked in the fish-scales. A row of these is sewn through the two holes spoken of previously, round the circumference, to represent the outer circle of petals, and within these a second circle is attached, overlapping the former, so as to conceal the threads by which they are attached, this is repeated till the center of the flower is reached, which is formed by a cluster of beads.

Yellow beads look remarkably well as they most nearly resemble the pollen of the natural flower.

Small leaves may be worked in fish-scales, but larger ones may be worked in ordinary embroidery, as should be stems.

Our illustration (Fig. 1) is intended for the top of a pincushion, the ground being of light colored satin. The stems are in gold thread, and the petals of the flowers and leaflets are each composed of one fish-scale. Where single scales are used, it is impossible to hide the stitch fastening them, but this may be rendered decorative by carrying the thread across the scale so as to resemble the center rib of the natural leaf.

FIG. 1

EXAMPLES OF FISH-SCALE EMBROIDERY

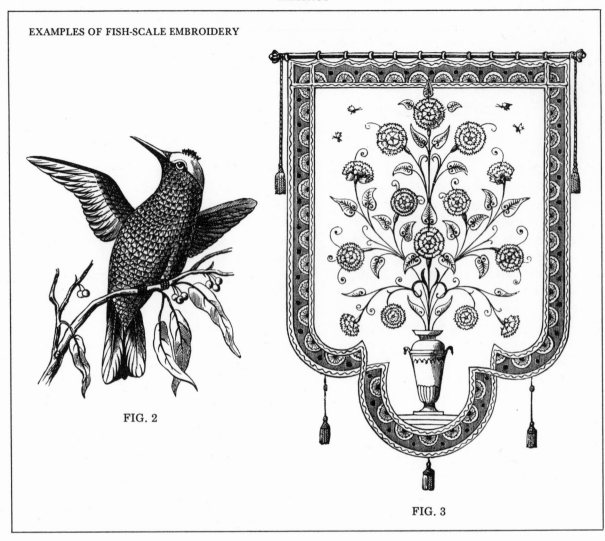

FIG. 2

FIG. 3

The design given in Fig. 2 may be applied to almost any article, and in combination with flowers, if desired. The eye of the bird will be a single bead, and the beak, legs, and some of the feathers, should be embroidered in silk.

The banner screen (Fig. 3) we have seen carried out in pink silk, with a green border, these colors being separated, and the whole work bound, with gold braid. The effect of the fish-scales upon the contrasting colors is very fine. It would be difficult to name a method of ornamentation which produces a more brilliant effect.

D'oyleys from Natural Foliage

To young ladies desirous of making presents to friends, by whom the work of their own hands is more likely to be appreciated than the most expensive article merely bought in a shop, or those at a loss what to contribute to bazaars or fancy fairs, we would suggest the beautiful and ingenious method of arranging ferns, or other gracefully shaped leaves as centers of a set of d'oyleys, where each can have a varied design, according to fancy or skill. The material should be cut into circles, as large as desired, with a plate as a pattern or in any other simple way.

The ferns or leaves selected should be flattened, by leaving them several days under pressure. The kinds which will be found most suitable, and have the best effect, are those of an open character, that is very much pierced or perforated, such as fern, wild geranium, oak, very young sprigs of vine, jessamine, or rose leaves; also the airy stems of grasses and harebells; these can easily be had in the country, and seaside visitors can attain the same results with sea-weed.

Having arranged the leaves tastefully in one of the cut circles, they may be held in their place by some very small pins standing perpendicularly. Dilute a quantity of Indian ink with water, then by dipping an old tooth-brush into it, and drawing it constantly backwards and forwards across the teeth of a small tooth comb, the d'oyley is covered all over with the finest spray, which produces the effect of a delicate granular ground, as fine as a highly finished lithograph, or even a photograph. Continue the process until it is of the required shade; never hurrying it, or taking too much ink on the brush, for fear of blots; nor even allowing the dots to be coarser at one time than another.

Fig. 1 is simple but appropriate in design, consisting merely of a few young vine leaves apparently laid over grasses, but in reality the grasses are laid over the vine; for the darkest leaves in the d'oyley are the first removed, the pure white always remaining till the ground is finished, which has generally the best effect when graduated or vignetted from the center

FIG. 1

FIG. 2

outwards. When satisfactorily concluded, it must be left a short time to dry; care also should be taken to allow it to be sufficiently dry between the removal of each layer of leaves. Then proceed with a pen, dipped in the same ink, to draw in the veins, &c., taken from the originals; the whole to be finished by a rose-colored silk fringe round the edge, or, by way of greater variety, each might have a different colored fringe.

Fig. 2 is a design which is capable of extensive adaptation to a great variety of tastes and requirements, inasmuch as, instead of the monogram here introduced, anyone may substitute their crest, armorial bearings, or a scroll with motto or name. This monogram was traced out on paper, afterwards cut out with scissors, and placed on first, the leaves arranged as in Fig. 1. The whole effect of this d'oyley could be reversed, by keeping it darker towards the outer edge, leaving the monogram upon a light ground in white, which could be tinted with color or gold at pleasure.

A D'OYLEY DESIGN

Conework

Pine cones are long familiar as Christmas decorations, and we were delighted to find Cassell suggesting less usual uses for them. Pine-cone scales create a charming effect when used in the manner described. They may be glued on almost any shape or surface, and their use is limited only by your patience and ingenuity.

We now propose to offer a few suggestions for adding to the decoration and attraction of home — the result chiefly arising from the experience of a rather lengthy residence in the "Far West." The young ladies of America understand well the art of turning everything to account, as well for ornament as for use. And what has hitherto by ourselves in England been considered as of no value, has by American taste been converted in pretty and useful articles, which make not only pleasing additions to one's own home, but provide an acceptable gift to a friend. Collecting the necessary materials will add much to the pleasure of a ramble in the woods. The best season of the year for procuring the requisites is in the autumn.

Make up a party to go off on an exploring expedition, and do not forget the children, for they as much as any will enjoy a day in the woods, coupled with the important commission of filling their little baskets. Make as varied a collection as possible of cones (or, as some say, "fir-apples"), the husks of the beech-nut, acorns, with and without the saucer part, oak apples, the cone of the cedar — and, indeed, of all coniferous trees, and nuts of different kinds. Even the knotted ends of small twigs mix in very nicely — the greater the variety the more pleasing the result. You will be surprised to learn how much lies at your feet of interest, beauty and use, which hitherto you have trodden upon as worthless, and which is available for domestic ornamentation.

Having collected a goodly stock of what the woods and lanes can give you, the next step is to prepare your supply for working. It is a good plan to sort the different things, putting each kind in a box or basket: this method will be found to expedite matters considerably. The large cones must be pulled to pieces — that is, strip off singly each scale, as they are needed for the foundation of the work. [You may need pliers for this.]

We will commence our lessons in conework by giving instructions for making a card-basket.

Conework Basket

Cut out of cardboard an oval about 9" by 7"; cut a smaller oval out of the center about 7½" by 5½". These form the bottom of the basket and the lip. Cut a 1½" strip of cardboard long enough to fit the circumference of the bottom; this is to be the sides of the basket. Cut another strip 1" by 11" for the handle. Tape the ends of the side strip together to form a loop and tape it to the bottom; tape the handle from end to end longways and then tape the lip to the upper edge of the basket. To produce the proper downward curve to the lip, cut four ½" wedges out of the lip and tape the edges together again.

You may now make the lining for the basket and handle, which should be of silk, satin, or paper, the color, of course, as taste dictates; some bright color looks best, such as amber, brilliant green, rose or blue.

Now for the conework.

Cut the root ends off of the cone scales and start to glue them on [the ends down], *commencing with a row around the bottom of the basket. Glue them as close together as possible. Add a second row, overlapping the first, the points of the scales down. Now*

FIG. 1

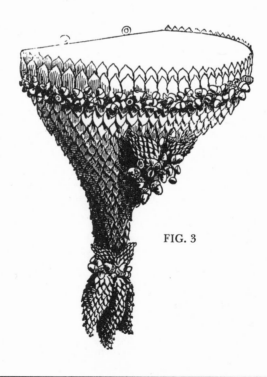

FIG. 2

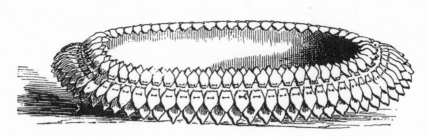

FIG. 3

glue a row of scales [points up] *around the lip of the basket; add a second row overlapping that as in Fig. 1. Fill the space between with small cones, nuts and acorns. Decorate the handle with a row of scales on either side and fill the center as before. Fig. 2 shows the finished basket.*

A variety of both useful and ornamental articles can be produced in this interesting and elegant work. One of the nicest things to be made in it is a bracket for the wall, which will have the appearance of carved oak. Fig. 3 will give you an idea of how a bracket looks when finishes; but the arrangement must rest with yourself — a cluster of acorns designed to represent a bunch of grapes looks well — and care must be taken to entirely cover the wood or foundation of the bracket. Very nice spill cups can be made in precisely the same way, using empty wooden boxes. Very handsome boxes for envelopes, stereoscopic slides, &c., can be made by tastefully covering empty boxes in which gentlemen's collars have been kept. In fact the cones may be applied to the decoration of a great variety of items which would be otherwise useless, and perhaps meet the fate of household rubbish generally.

Conework Pincushion

This is an easier project than the Conework Basket, and is a good way to start your experience with conework.

You will need:

Plastic margarine tub
White glue
Coarse sandpaper
Cardboard, 4" square
Velvet, 12" circle
Cotton wadding
Pine-cone scales, moss, etc. as described for other conework projects
Needle and thread

A small, sturdy plastic margarine tub makes a good base for this project. Roughen the outside of the tub slightly with coarse sandpaper to give a better gluing surface. Cut a round of cardboard to fit the outside bot-

tom of the tub and glue on to make a base. Glue on pine-cone scales as described for the basket, with points up for the top rows and points down at the base. The scales should project 1/3" above the top of the tub to hide the plastic. Decorate in the same way as the basket.

To make the pincushion: Cut a 12" circle of velvet; gather the edge with long stitches to make a bag. Take a ball of cotton, large enough to fill the tub to overflowing, and stuff the cotton into the velvet bag. Draw the gathering stitches tight to make a firm ball, and glue this, with the gathered side down, inside the tub so that only ¾" of the smoothly rounded velvet ball projects above the top of it. (We used moss-colored velvet and glued a circle of dried moss around the top of the tub, to hide any plastic that showed and to fill up any gap between the cone scales and velvet.)

To Remove Freckles — Take one ounce of lemon-juice, a quarter of a drachm of powdered borax, and a half drachm of sugar; mix, and let them stand a few days in a glass bottle, then rub it on the face and hands occasionally.

Imitation Coral Ornaments

Whilst writing our recent articles on paper flower-making it struck us that the alabaster vases and other ornaments generally purchased to show such bouquets were very costly, and beyond the reach of many of our readers. Not long ago we saw a beautiful and choice group of wax flowers, mounted under a glass shade, in a vase apparently of white coral, which had been made for a very trifling sum and without much trouble.

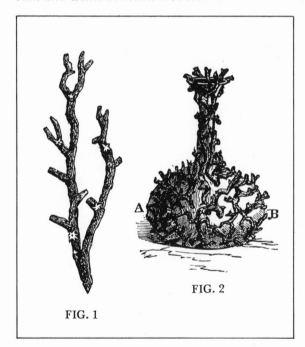

FIG. 1

FIG. 2

We weren't sure we would want to give house-room to an imitation coral vase in the shape of a wine bottle — or in any shape for that matter. But we took a small cobalt blue bowl, shaped the coral to circle the base and to creep up over the edge in several places, then set it on an oriental teak stand. We both liked our creation so well we had to flip a coin to see who would get to take it home.

Imitation Coral Vase

Take a long-necked wine bottle, with a rounded bowl, and with a coil of flexible wire

[we used pipe cleaners] *twine it all over to resemble coral, like Fig. 1, interlacing it every way. The spikes on the coral are merely loops twisted together. Fig. 2 shows the effect round the bottle. Make the top and bottom of the vase separately, divided at the line indicated by A and B, so that the bottle can be removed. Afterwards link this part together. Cover it all over with white Berlin wool [not necessary if you have used pipe cleaners]. Melt enough paraffin in a can set in hot water to dip the vase in, or pour the wax over it, melting it afresh as it congeals, till you have a good imitation of branch coral. When quite hard, fill the vase with dried moss. The flowers are placed in the usual way.*

Imitation Coral Basket

A basket constructed on the same principle is also very pretty. . . . The work may be varied by mixing vermillion oil paint with the wax, stirring it up just before pouring on the basket.

A CORAL BASKET

Imitation white coral shaped as a base for a small cobalt blue glass bowl.

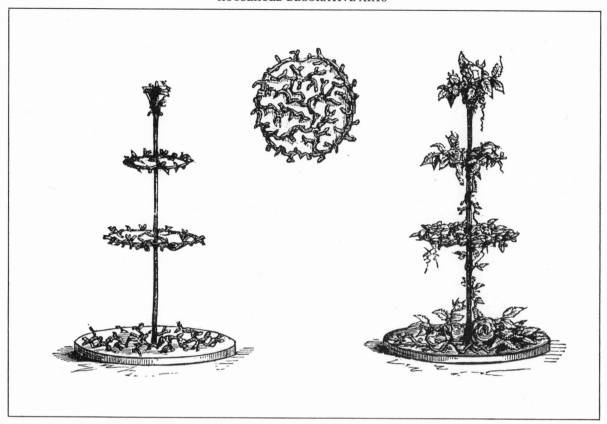

Table Ornaments

An ornament for the dinner-table is not difficult to contrive in the same way. Make three plates of different sizes in the coral; a slender stick is used for the stem, coated with wax. Get a circle of wood, half an inch thick, an inch wider than the coral stand at the base; cover it with crimson velvet, and put a wreath of ivy leaves round it; arrange a wreath round the stem. Put a little dried moss very lightly in each coral-plate at the center, leaving the edges free, and arrange flowers on them. The coral cup at the top can be made separate from the stand and added last. Fill these well with moss and flowers. Fig. 3 shows the stand; Fig. 4 one of the plates. The cup at the top can be made over a jelly-glass. Fig. 5 shows the stand dressed. White coral is best for this purpose.

Souvenirs and Tasteful Trifles

Judging by Cassell, it would seem that sentimental gifts were exchanged by Victorian ladies upon any and all occasions. Since Papa controlled the purse strings and a good deal of pin money went into just that, the majority of these tokens were, perforce, homemade. Surely, favorite uncles must have owned two lifetimes supplies of Berlin wool slippers, knitted mufflers, and conework humidors.

The following items are only a fraction of the possible ways to express one's tender feelings.

Gentleman's Toilette Case

Take a piece of moire and of silk the same color and size. These should be cut large enough to hold the necessities; a strop, a pair of ivory-mounted razors, a box brush in ivory, and ivory soap-box, a pair of nail scissors, a penknife, a button-hook, an ivory tooth-brush case, an ivory nail-brush case, and a tongue-scraper. A small "housewife," with thread, needles, and buttons, and a scent-case of white silk may also be placed in the pocket, see Fig. 1. Run from end to

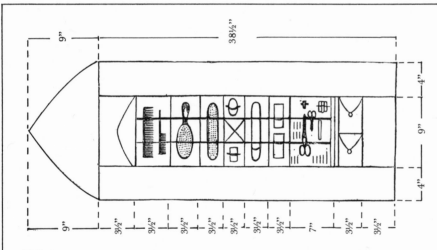

The case when closed

FIG. 1 A gentleman's toilet case would take about 1 1/3 yards of 36" fabric

Surmount the monogram with a crest or coronet, if the gentleman for whom the case is designed has either.

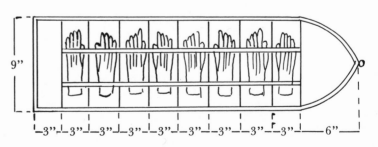

A lady's glove case made in the same way

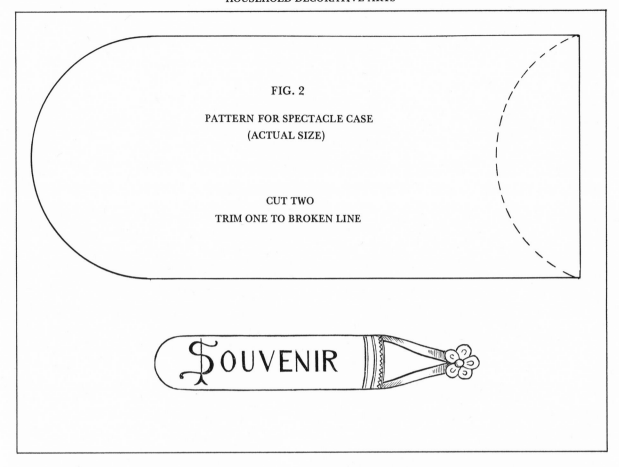

FIG. 2

PATTERN FOR SPECTACLE CASE
(ACTUAL SIZE)

CUT TWO
TRIM ONE TO BROKEN LINE

end of the silk lining two strips of elastic, stitch down at the right intervals to contain the fittings. Add pockets, as shown, with bound edges. Tack the lining now to the moire back. If this is to have initials on it, they should be worked first on the part which will form the back when rolled up.

When the lining and back are tacked together, cut the flaps of silk, bind three sides of them; lay them in the way they are to be folded when the case is closed; tack the raw edges to the edges of the case, and bind the whole with ribbon all round; add a ribbon to tie it closed.

Spectacle Case

This is to be made of velvet. Cut one of each shape of stout cardboard as in Fig. 2. Cut two pieces of velvet the same shape but larger. Tack the velvet in an embroidery frame and embroider the word Souvenir and the border on one piece, and a monogram and a border on the other, the letters first

raised then worked over in satin stitch. Cover each piece of card with a piece of the velvet, drawing the edges of the velvet close by catching it across and across with a needle and thread on the wrong side of the card. Cut some silk a bit larger than the card, turn in the edges, and sew it on as a lining. Next sew the two pieces of the case together neatly, with silk thread that matches the velvet. Suspend it to two pieces of ribbon uniting in a knot of bows, under which there is a long hook. The hook is to fasten the case to the waist.

Lady's Shoe Tidy

This is a very useful and pretty article in a bedroom, and it is very simple to make. Cut two 36" circles of stout fabric, one a pretty pattern and one a plain color. With the right sides together, sew them round leaving only a small opening through which to turn them. Turn them right side out, press well, and blind stitch the opening. Then divide the circle exactly in six sections, folding it very carefully, and creasing the folds strongly with a hot iron. Open it. Place the end of a stout hook handled cane in the center of the circle. Nail the fabric to the cane along one crease. Use a number of small upholstery tacks for this. Continue to nail the creases to the cane all the way around. See Fig. 3. Hang over the clothing bar and fill with shoes.

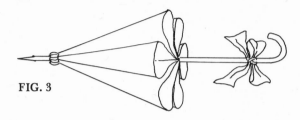

FIG. 3

Decorated Needle-Book

To make a very pretty needle-book, cut eight cards the shape of Fig. 4. Decorate four of them with watercolors like the illustration (Fig. 5) or paste flower prints on them. To each decorated piece bind a plain one, by means of a very narrow strip of gold paper, about 3/8" wide. Clip the paper every 1/16" where it bends around a curve. Drill a hole at the bottom of each, and sew all together with a large bead, so as to form a fan; or fasten with a loop and tassel as shown in Fig. 5. In the hollow at the top of each piece, slip a piece of cardboard cut as Fig. 6, to which a paper of needles has been affixed.

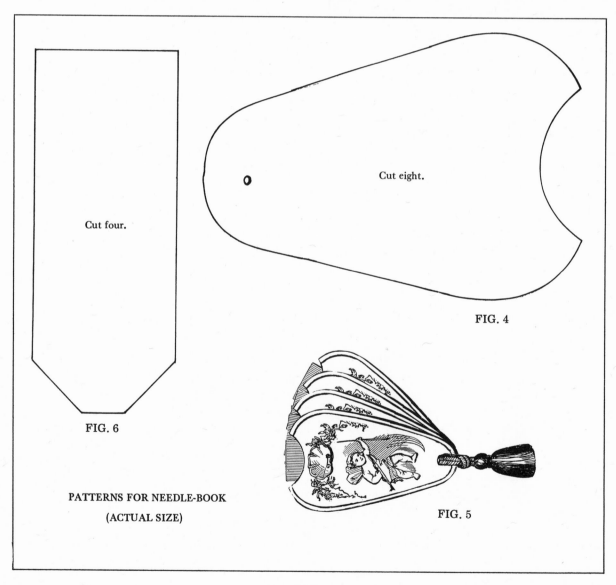

Cut four.

Cut eight.

FIG. 4

FIG. 6

PATTERNS FOR NEEDLE-BOOK

(ACTUAL SIZE)

FIG. 5

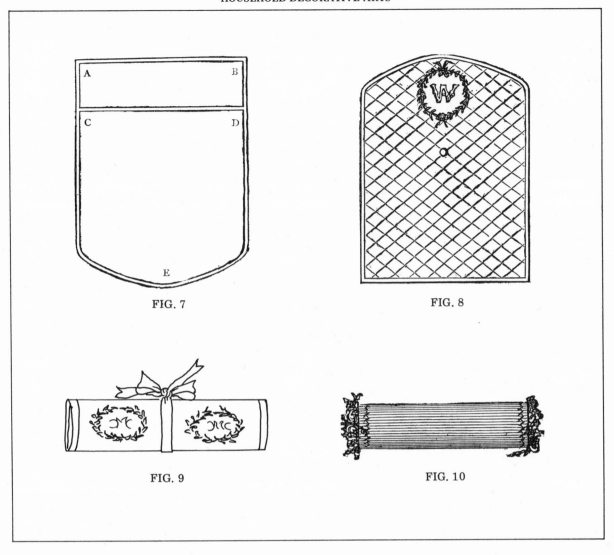

FIG. 7

FIG. 8

FIG. 9

FIG. 10

Music Wrappers

It is very easy and cheap to make ordinary music wrappers. Procure a small piece of oil cloth. Lay a piece of music on it, and cut the cloth larger all round so as to cover the music well. The music should be placed in the wrapper with the back, or folded part, level from A to B, Fig. 7. Cut another piece for the pocket from the surplus. Bind the edge of the pocket, C to D, with binding. Then tack it to the case. Begin at A, bind the two together to B, and go on binding all round. Put on two long strings of binding at E. Roll it up and tie the strings in a bow as shown in Fig. 9. It is a good plan to write the name and address of the owner in large letters on the wrong side of the case, so that if lost, any honest person finding it would restore it.

To make an elegant case for a musical friend, see Fig. 8. It is of azure blue satin, lined with quilted white silk, and monogrammed. Or instead of quilting, work in white satin stitch an appropriate motto, such as —

May harmony as sweet as this,
lull thy gentle heart in bliss.

Fig. 10 is another elegant wrapper, designed to carry two or three songs to a party or concert. Make it of pink silk, and when bound tack to the edge a fringe of white marabout.

Take a number of small artificial flowers, leaves and short grass: tack them in a row to each edge, and then run them over neatly in a second piece of ribbon, turning up the wire edges inside. In making the pocket, some powder-scent should have been previously dropped between the lining. When rolled up, a bouquet is presented.

FIG. 11   PATTERN FOR AN EMBROIDERED AND BEADED KEY BAG
(ACTUAL SIZE)

Key Bag

A key bag is very pretty and useful, and most young housewives would appreciate the convenience, for it is not fit to carry heavy keys in a dress pocket, where, too, they are apt to get entangled with other things. Take some velvet, cut it by the pattern in Fig. 11. Two pieces are wanted. Tack them in a work frame. The leaves are to be embroidered with white chalk beads, gold, and pearl beads. When the embroidery is finished, line the velvet with silk, tack the pieces together, and bind all round the edges with ribbon. Suspend it by two ribbons and a bow, behind which is a very large, strong hook. Sew an eye to the waist band, or skirt of the dress close to the waist, on the left side in front of the hip, and hang the key-bag from it.

Working in Hair

The Victorian's extreme sentimentality about hair — hair brooches, hair bracelets, hair pictures and mourning wreaths — seems strange and slightly macabre today. It was, perhaps, an outgrowth of the cult of mourning, inspired by Victoria's forty years of demonstrative bereavement. Since hairwork was so popular in the era, we wanted at least to attempt one of Cassell's relatively simple hair projects. We were left with a feeling of wonder, not untinged with horror, at the patience and hours that must have been expended on more elaborate hair ornaments. Examples of these are avidly sought after by collectors of Victoriana. Here is Cassell on the wonders of hair:

The imperishable nature of human hair, and the great brilliancy and beauty which it retains long after it has been severed, even after the person to whom it once belonged has passed away, have always rendered it one of the most cherished mementoes of absent or departed friends.

Hair Brooches

The art of working this material into designs for brooches or other ornaments is far from being a difficult one, the chief requisites being neatness of hand, and some little patience. It is, in fact, so simple that we may well wonder at its being so rarely practiced; especially when we consider how liable those persons who entrust the cherished hair of a relation or friend to professed workers are to be deceived by having ready-made devices similar in color, but manufactured from the hair of some person with whom they are probably, wholly unacquainted, substituted for it. Of course, in all hair jewellery or ornament the chief value is a sentimental one, and when any doubt

exists of the hair itself being genuine all real interest attaching to the article is lost.

In some more complicated devices a pretty effect may be obtained, as is shown in our designs, by using hair of two or more shades or colors, which will sometimes increase the sentimental interest of the ornament, as, for instance, when the hair of. . . mother and child. . . is used together.

Devices may be formed of hair previously gummed to paper such as those we give as examples in Fig. 1 and 2. In these, it will be seen that the design should first be roughly sketched and the different parts cut from the paper, then covered with hair. and gummed separately into their places. In Fig. 1, the two hearts are prepared to be made from the hair of two persons, as of husband and wife, while the lighter hair of their child may be employed for the crown and border. In Fig. 2, the star may be formed of the lighter hair of the lady, the darker part from that of the gentleman. Halved seed pearls are gummed on to outline and ornament the design.

FIG. 1

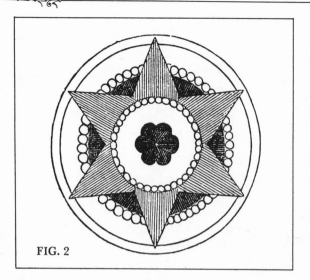

FIG. 2

A somewhat different process to that which we have described will be required in carrying out the mourning brooch shown in Fig. 3. The central stems of the bay-wreath are formed of hair, not fixed beforehand to paper, but simply dipped in the solution of gum, and then carefully arranged in its place on lines previously sketched upon the background. The leaves in this brooch are formed of hair fixed upon paper; the berries are halved pearls; the letters of the inscription should be carefully put in with Indian ink.

Flowers, of which we give an example in Fig. 4, are also formed of hair on paper.

The purpose to which hair-work is usually devoted is that of jewellery, though designs thus made are sometimes mounted and framed, in the same manner as photographs and miniatures, for hanging upon walls.

Sentimental Ornament

To begin with, you must be very sure that the prospective recipient of this rather outré token of affection has a sense either of history or of humor. For the design we used the Prince's feather, then framed it with gold paper lace and a rather crude little Victorian picture frame. The kindest thing we can say about the results is that it's interesting.

You will need:

Oval frame of embossed gold paper 1½" to 2"
Narrow border of embossed gold paper
Corner motifs of embossed gold paper
Silk or satin fabric in two colors
Small picture frame (shadow box if possible)
Cardboard
Tiny pearl beads
Hair
Waxed paper
Needle and thread
Transparent tape, double-faced
White glue and brush
Round wooden toothpicks

FIG. 3   FIG. 4

A treasured lock of hair displayed on a background
of silk and gold embossed paper in a small gilded frame.

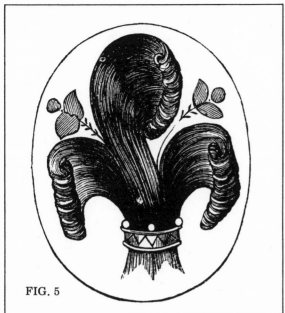

FIG. 5

On a piece of waxed paper lay out three pieces of double-faced tape approximately ½" long. Lay a toothpick on each, parallel and close to one edge of the tape. Take a small bundle of hair, about 2" long. Cut it square on one end and press it to the tape at right angles to the toothpick. Prepare two more bundles in the same manner. See Fig. 6.

Start to roll the toothpick toward the hair until the hair on the tape is just into the roll. Holding the toothpick firmly against the hair so that it will not pull off the tape, brush white glue, slightly diluted with water, over the hair. Continue to roll the hair on the toothpick and pull the curl to the right or left to form the plumes as shown in Fig. 5. Tape the hair and the toothpick in position and allow to dry.

When the glue is completely dry, remove the tape and toothpicks gently so as not to

pull the curls of hair apart. Trim all the loose or non-conforming hairs away with sharp scissors.

Cut two pieces of cardboard slightly larger than the opening of the oval paper frame. Cover one with silk or satin by sewing it across the back. Then glue on the other to cover the stitches. Glue the paper frame onto the silk. Arrange the three plumes of hair in their proper positions and glue them together at the base with a narrow band of gold paper. Split two small pearl beads and glue three halves in place; then glue the entire thing to the silk. Ours protrudes over the paper frame.

Cover a piece of cardboard to fit the picture frame with silk of another color, and edge the cardboard with gold paper border and fancy corner motifs; affix the medallion with the hair in the center and frame it. A shadow-box frame is best as it will protect your memento from dust without crushing the hair.

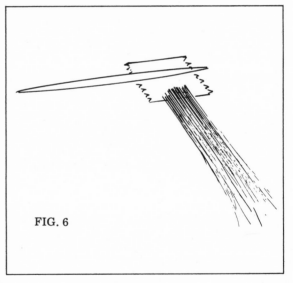

FIG. 6

Colored Transparencies

This was not a new pastime. For as long as paper has been in common use, idle young ladies, with scissors in hand, have found artistic excuses for wasting it. Some of Jane Austen's characters had been "making paper flowers and wasting gold paper" and putting transparencies in their windows at the turn of the nineteenth century.

Trace the subjoined design [enlarged to about 5" by 7"] *on a large square of moderately stout white cardboard,* [it should be opaque], *or instead of a square, say a piece fourteen inches by eleven. The tracing should be as light as possible. With a sharp knife cut around the entire outline, leaving the vase and flowers attached only at the base A to A.* [Then cut along all the black lines in the design.] *It will be perceived that none of the pieces are entirely severed from one another, every one being joined at some place to the*

whole. Color the background portion of the card indicated by the dotted line E to G on the opposite side of the card from which it is to be viewed. From D to E, with a smear of strong carmine, from C to D with sap green, from B to C with carmine, and from F to B with cobalt blue. The rest of the area from F to G should be colored a paler tint of green. The part round the vase is left uncolored. Let the colors be both deep and full. When completed, bend the group of flowers and vase the very least bit possible backwards through the aperture. In this state hold it up towards the light of a candle or single gas-burner [or tape it in a window], *the colored part turned towards the light.*

The colors on the back of the card are reflected onto the uncolored cutout bouquet and give a beautiful effect.

DESIGN FOR A TRANSPARENCY

Watercolor Drawing on Wood

England is universally acknowledged to be the fatherland of water-color drawing; but . . . we have left to our neighbors on the continent the credit of applying it to household purposes — domesticating it, as it were. It is a principle with us to hide from sight every possible piece of plain wood; whether it be the floor with a carpet, or a toilette-box with chintz and lace. They, on the contrary, inlay with various colored woods in fancy patterns the former; and the latter, if the polished grain of the wood be not sufficiently attractive, is ornamented with designs in water-colors, or tinted in sepia, and then polished. Articles of the toilette are either bought in this state, or (which is far preferable, as we want to inculcate in the present paper) are painted at home, and thus afford "amusement and instruction hand in hand." For we contend that the education of the artistic feelings and taste cannot be too earnestly cultivated.

Before describing the accompanying illustration, we proceed to give some general hints as to the modus operandi. The wood chosen for coloring should be of as hard a quality with as little grain as possible; the former to reduce to a minimum the probability of the color running, which, however, it will do under any circumstances if laid on too moist; and the grain, if prominent and handsome, destroying the effect of artificial ornament, Nature being in that, as in everything else, unapproachable.

Salad Servers

We give here a suitable subject for the style of art in a salad-fork and spoon. . . . The design is first drawn in outline with a good pencil, but not so as to injure the surface of the wood. The spaces, in the design, shown white are painted in with white, the black portions done with India ink; while the shaded areas are tinted with sepia. The remaining portion is either left the color of the wood, or in the case of a decided grain, is colored with a warm grey. When thoroughly dry the pencil lines are gone over with a fine mathematical pen and India ink. Should it be found necessary to go over the black portions a second time, it should be done before these final lines are drawn, as they give a finish and decisiveness to the outlines not otherwise attainable. When dry, apply varnish [clear spray acrylic finish]. This is almost a new art in England, but deserves cultivation.

SALAD SPOON AND FORK
ORNAMENTED

Bonbonnières

The accompaning illustrations represent further and more advanced specimens of the manner in which we may apply this art. Fig. 1 represents a bonbonnière made with a frame work of cane-laths with panels of lime-wood. Fig. 2 is a small toilette-box, made entirely of maple and ornamented with painting. The design for the top of both Figs. 1 and 2 is given about full size in Fig. 3. [See page 159.] With the exercise of a little ingenuity with which we credit our readers, these designs can be adapted to any size or shape required, for it will rarely happen that the same article that we give is on hand.

Don't we all wish we had these intriguing little boxes on hand. We liked the bonbonnière so well that we copied it — in a somewhat simplified form. Rather than attempt the fine carpentry needed to make a wooden box this size, we made it in cardboard with the same technique used in making the Shell Box described earlier, and covered it with a wood veneer paper.

You will need:

Cardboard, about 8" by 10", 1/8" thick
Razor knife
Thin bamboo, ¼" (dried stalks from the garden)
Wood veneer paper (not plastic-coated)
Decorative paper for lining
Artist's watercolor or acrylic paints
India ink and drawing pen
Gloss black enamel
Masking tape
Scissors
Glue
Tracing paper
Cotton fabric

Cut two pieces of cardboard the size and shape of Fig. 3 for the bottom and lid of the box. Cut six rectangular side pieces, each 2" wide and 1½" high. Tape the sides and the bottom of the box together.

Cut a strip of veneer paper approximately 2¾" by 13", glue it around the outside of the box (bend the excess paper neatly to the inside of the box, and under at the bottom edge). Start this at one corner, and trim neatly at the end to finish at the same corner with a tiny overlap.

Cut a piece of veneer paper to fit the outside bottom and glue in place. Cut veneer paper ½" wider all round than the top and glue it to the top, notch each corner, and wrap the excess paper carefully over the edges to the inside.

Trace whatever design you like on the top and color it as suggested by Cassell.

Cut six bamboo legs, each 2 3/8" long. Cut them so a joint on the bamboo makes a foot. Make a horizontal cut half way through

FIG. 1　　　　　　　　　　FIG. 2

A frivolous little bonbonnière of simulated wood with bamboo legs and edging, and decorated with a painted design.

each leg 1½" from the top, then split the bamboo in half lengthwise down to this point, see Fig. 4. Glue the cut side of the bamboo to a corner of the box, while resting the bottom of the box on the shelf created by the uncut portion. Use small pieces of split bamboo to finish the top and bottom edges of the sides, and cut slits in six 2" pieces of bamboo to slip over the six edges of the lid. Miter the corners to make the bamboo fit evenly. Before gluing the bamboo to the box, paint or spray all pre-cut pieces with black enamel.

Hinge the lid to the box on the inside by gluing on a strip of cotton fabric. (See directions for making a Shell Box on page 52.) Line the inside of the box and lid with decorative paper.

FIG. 4

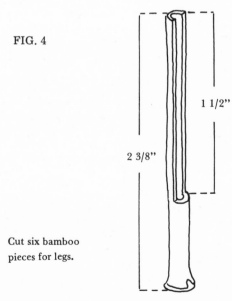

1 1/2"

2 3/8"

Cut six bamboo
pieces for legs.

Skeleton Leaves

Descriptions of and instructions for making these intriguing ornaments appear not only in Cassell, but in many other Victorian books. All agree as to the method to be used, but so far we have had little success in making them. We do know that it is possible, as we have seen the finished product in museums. They are produced naturally, however, and we were lucky enough to find a cache of skeleton leaves beside a stream bed. Pressed and arranged, they make a lovely, "fairylike" bouquet.

Here are Cassell's instructions if you wish to experiment. Good luck!

The subject of this paper is one of many means of household decoration, but it certainly deserves a high rank among the adornments of the home of taste. The object in view is to remove all the fleshy parts of the leaves, retaining intact the veins. The simplest process is by maceration. Lay the leaves in water until they become partially decayed, allowing the skin and fleshy matter to become decomposed, and stopping the process before it attacks the fibers.

Use only perfect, mature leaves. July is usually the best month to gather them. A good plan is to hold the leaf up to the light, when any defect is generally readily seen.

A large number of leaves should be gathered; they are then to be placed in a small tub, or pan, covered with water, and put in the open air, exposed to the sun; the loss of water by evaporation being made up as required. After two weeks they may be examined at intervals, say twice a week, but oftener if the weather is warm; and any leaves that are found to be soft and pulpy may be removed to a basin of clean water.

A word as to removing the leaves; cause the leaves to float, then slip a card underneath, and lift it from the water, otherwise they are apt to fall apart.

The maceration is the most unpleasant part of the whole business, for when the vessel is disturbed for the purpose of taking out the decaying leaves, the stench is often unbearable, and the leaves look so filthy that it does not seem possible that such beautiful results can be arrived at by these means.

When the leaves are collected in a basin of clean water, the operation of cleaning commences. It will be necessary to have at least two brushes, one a soft camel's hair, one stiffer brush; an old tooth-brush does very well. A leaf should be floated on to a card, lifted out of the water, and gently brushed with the soft brush until the skin is cleaned off; then slip the card and leaf in the water, and lift it out with the other side of the leaf uppermost. This side must be gently brushed to clean off the skin, when usually the fleshy parts will wash out as loose green colored matter, leaving the clean skeleton on the card. Sometimes small portions of green matter will adhere to the skeleton, when the soft brush must be again applied; if that does not move it, use the hard brush, but always with the greatest possible care; and it must never be used with a sweeping motion, but always with a downward tapping motion, or the skeleton will inevitably be destroyed.

Another basin of clean water should be ready at hand, and the card with the cleaned skeleton should be immersed, and the skeleton left in the water while other leaves are cleaned.

After that, again float them on to a clean card, taking care that they are as flat and as near their natural shape as it is possible to get them. When nicely arranged on a card, lift them out and let them drain; dry them as quickly as possible. They are now sufficiently strong to bear handling with ordinary care. Leaves containing tan cannot be done by this process, for the tan resists decomposition.

After being dried, they may be mounted in various ways, according to taste; but being pale in color, their appearance is much improved by a dark background; so that, if arranged as a bouquet under a shade, the bot- *tom should be covered with black velvet, and some delicate leaves displayed about it. If forming a group to hang against a wall, the back should be covered with black velvet.*

The Water Bouquet

We tried these bouquets with great success. They are easy to make, and just a bit out of the ordinary. Where Cassell uses a stone to hold the flowers, we used florist's clay. Practice with a few flowers, a tumbler, and a saucer. It works!

An extremely pretty variation from ordinary floral arrangements . . . consists of flowers, leaves, &c. immersed in water beneath a glass basin turned bottom upwards, and owes its peculiar beauty to the sparkling and frostlike appearance which vegetable forms assume under such circumstances, and to the illusive and fairylike effect caused by the refraction of light, and the magnifying power of the combined glass and water.

Glass shades of any size or shape are among the best receptacles in which to make the water-bouquet, but any plain glass may be made to serve. In addition, a plate or dish has to be provided sufficiently large to admit of the edge of the glass shade or basin resting smoothly on its flat inner surface.

In the center of the plate or dish the flowers are arranged; they may be tied to a stone to hold them in place, which must then be concealed by moss or leaves, so that everything may appear as though growing naturally beneath the water.

When the general arrangement is completed, a vessel full of water must be prepared, sufficiently large to admit of both plate and glass cover being submerged in it. In the bottom of this vessel the plate with the bouquet must be placed, and some further arrangement of the latter will now in most cases be necessary, to restore any leaves or petals which *may have been displaced by the action of the water, and to make such slight alterations as will be suggested by their effect when seen through the new element, and care must be taken that nothing projects so far towards the edges of the plate as to touch those parts on which the edge of the glass will have to rest.*

When everything is satisfactorily arranged, take the glass shade, and put it into the water sideways, so as to leave no air within it, and then put it in its position upon the plate. The whole may then be lifted from the tub, and the shade will remain full of water, which as there will be no atmospheric pressure from within, will not flow out, though it will be well to leave a little water in the bottom of the plate round the edge of the glass, to keep it thoroughly air-tight.

Any person who makes a water bouquet for the first time, will be surprised to find how small a number of flowers or other objects are necessary, apparently, to fill the glass. This is owing to the magnifying power of the convex glass filled with water.

These things are not in their greatest perfection immediately after they are made. On the second day the flowers and leaves become covered, especially at their edges, with minute air bubbles, which impart to them a beautifully frosted appearance.

In summer flowers will of course be the materials used in making these decorations. In winter the leaves and berries of holly, arbutus, &c., look exceedingly pretty; and for those staying at the sea-side a charming bouquet may be made with sea-weeds and shells.

Picture Checkerboards

A very pretty checkerboard may be made by arranging on any kind of white wood alternate squares of small oil prints, or the prints may be alternated with squares of white paper. They must be cut and fitted with extreme precision, and very thoroughly fixed at the corners, by means of a strong glue. A border should be placed round; a light-brown scroll pattern by no means massive. The oil prints should be of one kind and of one tone of color, either light or dark. Landscapes may be chosen to decorate the board, or figures, or even heads. Oblongs may be used, if wide enough for the pieces to stand upon, but squares are better.

Children's Checkerboard

We liked the idea of a checkerboard made of cut-out prints, but made some changes in Cassell's plan. Our board is made of cardboard covered with blue and white gingham trimmed with matching ribbon, and the squares are decorated with Kate Green-

away figures. A set of wooden checkers painted blue and white, and a small tin box to hold them, painted blue and decorated with Kate Greenaway figures, completes the set.

You will need:

Heavy cardboard, 18" square
Checked gingham ¾ of a yard of 48" wide with 1/8" checks
Grosgrain ribbon, 2 yards of ¼" wide
Thirty-two pictures, ¾" square
Découpage finish and brush
Clear spray acrylic finish
Wooden checkers
Small box (tin or wood) to hold checkers
Masking tape
Glue
Waxed paper
White spray enamel
Colored spray enamel (to match the color of gingham)

Cut a 20" square of gingham. Center the cardboard on the fabric, lining up the edges so that the gingham is exactly squared on all sides. Tape to hold it in place. Mark the position of the board with light pencil lines. Remove the cardboard and give it an even coat of découpage finish, re-position on the fabric, and press down firmly. Turn over again and glue down the 1" margin all around, keeping the corners as flat as possible.

Cut a second 20" square of gingham, turn under a 1/8" hem all around and iron flat, making sure the fabric is exactly squared. Apply a coat of finish to the back of the board and position the gingham on it. Once the gingham is fixed firmly, give one side a generous coat of finish and allow it to dry on a piece of waxed paper. When it is no longer sticky, turn it and give the other side a coat of finish. When both sides are dry, press it, between sheets of waxed paper, under a weight for several hours to correct any warping.

A children's checkerboard covered with blue and white
gingham, and decorated with Kate Greenaway figures.
It has its own box to hold the blue and white counters.

Cut thirty-two exact 1¾" squares of decorative prints: ours were plain white paper with Kate Greenaway stickers pasted on them. Mark the placement of the squares lightly in pencil along one side, leaving a 2" border all around the outside edge of the board.

Give the playing area a coat of découpage finish and position the decorative squares. Border the checkerboard area with four bands of ¼" grosgrain ribbon, allowing them to cross at the corners and cutting them flush with the edge of the board. Give the entire board a coat of découpage finish and allow it to dry

until clear. Continue to apply coats of découpage finish until you have from eight to ten layers. Wet-sand it and apply a coat of clear spray acrylic finish to seal it, as described in Furniture Decorated with Chintz (see page 82).

Paint sixteen of the wooden checkers with white enamel, and sixteen with colored enamel. Paint the box with colored enamel. Decorate the box with cutout pictures as desired, then finish with two or three coats of clear acrylic.

To Destroy Flies — Strong green tea, sweetened well, and set in saucers about the places where they are most numerous, will attract and destroy them. This plan is much to be preferred to the use of those horrible fly-papers, which catch the poor insects alive, cruelly torturing them while starving them to death.

Scrapscreen

The happiest part of Cassell's description of a proper nursery is "it should be light and airy, for children immured in gloomy apartments never have a ruddy bloom." The rest sounds wholesome but uninteresting.

The bare necessities [of furniture] *are all that should be admitted, the fittings should be few and washable, plain chintz to be preferred. . . . It would perhaps shock most people to tell them that the very best walls for a nursery are those which are simply plastered and whitewashed. The whitewash may be renewed every year at trifling cost, doing away with the harbor for fleas and more objectionable insects.*

If this is the way English nurseries were in fact, no wonder that a scrapscreen (a large version of a scrapbook) figures in so many descriptions of them. It would have been the one cheerful note in an otherwise drab room, and letting the children make one would keep them out of mischief.

Many useful and amusing occupations can be recommended for long evenings, and among such occupations we reckon especially those which result in the production of something at once permanant and ornamental.

Preparing scraps with which to cover a screen is an employment that fills up a good deal of spare time, entails no mental exertion, and may be done at small expense, beyond that for the mere frame of the screen with a simple covering of black paper. It would be useless to lay down any very accurate rules where so much must be left to taste, and the work admits of endless variety.

There are different ways of covering a screen. The first and simplest, as regards preparation, is the sticking on of prints from which the margins have been removed. Pictures for such purposes may be collected from various friends and laid on according to taste. Some-times all kinds of pictures, of all shapes and sizes are arranged as it were pell-mell, every cranny and nook being filled up. At other times they are arranged in studied confusion, as in Fig. 1. [See page 171.] *This requires materials all of one size. All the corners and angles* [of the screen] *left uncovered by this arrangement, must be filled in with portions of pictures, for which torn ones will come in useful.*

Another way of covering a screen is by cutting out the outlines of prints and sticking them on. Comic arrangements may be got in this way, as for instance, cut out an umbrella and place it as if held by a duck, or transfix a pair of spectacles to the countenence of a lion.

Pictures that are all square may be arranged in stars as in Fig. 2, or if cut out in diamond shape may be arranged as in Fig. 3.

After pasting thé pictures firmly down in the pattern chosen, the entire screen should be varnished.

A tall folding screen is often a convenient addition to a child's room. It offers an attractive way to hide a cluttered corner, and is a good way to display a child's treasured collection of pictures.

We painted a two-panel screen white, then, adapting Cassell's arrangement shown in Fig. 3, made a giant starburst centered on the fold of the screen. We cut brightly colored pictures from magazines, mounted them on diamonds cut from construction paper, and glued them on the screen.

Our screen measured 54" by 72"; the starburst design is 40" in diameter and took thirty-six diamonds, each 5¾" by 10". The plan we give here is for a screen of those dimensions, but you can use one of any size so long as the design is centered, and enlarged or reduced to fit.

A two-panel screen for a child's room decorated with
a sunburst of colorful pictures.

FIG. 1

FIG. 2

FIG. 3

You will need:

Folding screen
White semigloss enamel
Pictures (from magazines or greeting cards)
Construction paper, assorted colors
White glue
Clear spray acrylic finish
Pushpins

Paint the screen white (or other color, as desired). Cut thirty-six diamonds as shown in Fig. 4 from construction paper in various colors. On a table, lay out the thirty-six diamonds in the design, arranging the colors harmoniously. Plan and cut your pictures so they will be upright on the screen.

Trim the pictures to fit the diamonds, leaving a ¼" margin of construction paper showing as a border, then glue them neatly on the diamonds.

Starting from the center point of the screen, begin to arrange the diamonds. Use pushpins to hold them in place until you have the entire design laid out, because you may want to move the pictures to give a better effect. When the design is complete, remove the pins and glue each diamond in place. If you want to add a narrow ribbon border around the edge of the screen do so at this point; glue it in place. When the glue is dry, finish the screen with two or three coats of clear spray acrylic finish.

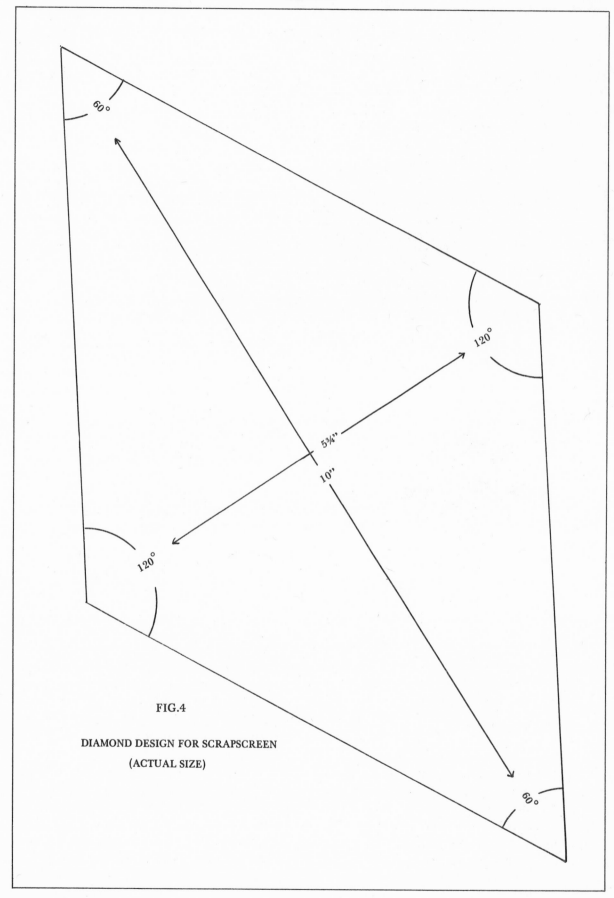

FIG.4

DIAMOND DESIGN FOR SCRAPSCREEN
(ACTUAL SIZE)

Easter Eggs

Very pretty articles for presents can be made out of Easter eggs. In the northern counties of England the reciprocal giving of Easter eggs is a general custom and expressive of good-will, and everyone vies with the other to produce the prettiest.

Get scraps of ribbon of all sorts, old and new — dark, bright colors are best. Wrap them round and round the eggs and sew them up tight. Boil the eggs as many hours as you like. Take them out and unroll them. Most of them will be dyed like the ribbons. They do not all succeed. Of course only one colored ribbon is used to one egg; although a ribbon in itself variegated often produces a beautiful egg, two colored ribbons wrapped around an egg would be likely to create a confusion of color.

An Easter egg forms a still prettier gift if you scratch on it landscapes or comic figures, or kindly mottoes, executed neatly with a sharp penknife. We have seen many of these scratched eggs made beautiful works of art. Choose a brown, crimson, or violet dyed egg for this purpose, or at least one rather dark in color, as the device appears in white. Fig. 1 is a guide for a landscape.

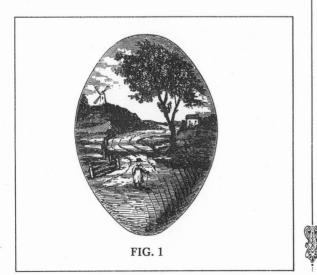

FIG. 1

Another way of making Easter eggs is to boil them very hard; cut each egg in half; remove the meat. Gum on a piece of silk, satin or ribbon, with the top drawn up previously like a bag, with a frill and strings, put a strip of prettily embossed gold paper over the join of the silk and the egg. Fill the bag with sweetmeats or any little present you wish to make — such as a ring or a thimble, laid at the top of sugarplums. Eggs dyed may be cut in half, and then scratched prettily and a bag added. Fig. 2 illustrates the egg-bag; Fig. 3 is a second design for a frill.

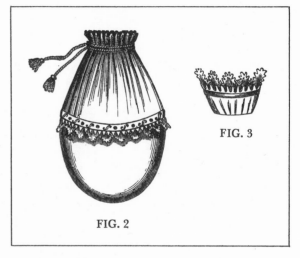

FIG. 3

FIG. 2

Or boil and cut off three-quarters of the egg in the way described; paint over the shell with white of egg. When that is dry, draw a garland, or device, or motto surrounded with flowers, using watercolors and a fine brush. If all the colors are well mixed with flake-white before using them, the effect will be superior. Have a silk or satin bag ready to gum on when the drawing on the egg is quite dry. Those who are not skilled in drawing can ornament Easter eggs by means of garlands and small scraps of prints for decalcomanie.

Another way of making an Easter egg is to boil one very hard; cut it in half length-

ways; bind the edge of each half with gold paper; gum a ribbon across the hollow of each, leaving ends at both sides. Sew two ends together in a bow to make a hinge; fill the egg with sweetmeats, or some little gift, and having closed it, tie the ribbon ends.

Take an old strawberry basket and [glue] it all over thickly with moss, like a bird's nest. Or make a cardboard basket and cover it with moss. Put three or more eggs of different colors in the nest. This is a pretty present.

We tried all of these Easter eggs. The ones we did with ribbons, "did not succeed," but perhaps we didn't try hard enough. (We would be reluctant to eat any eggs colored by this means, as the dyes used for ribbon are probably not meant for human consumption.)

The scratched eggs are attractive, especially if done, as Mr. Cassell suggests, on very dark-colored eggs.

We liked the eggs cut lengthways and tied with ribbons best. The ribbons must be very, very narrow so that they don't overpower the egg.

Acrylic paints work very well on eggshell and don't require the coat of egg-white beforehand.

To Preserve Flowers — Take a jar sufficiently large to contain the flower to be preserved, and in the bottom place a lump of clay or some similar substance, in which the flower must be stuck upright. Then pour in carefully fine dry sand till the flower is completely embedded in it. This must be done very slowly and cautiously, so as not to disturb the leaves of the flower. Dried in this manner, flowers preserve their form and much of their colour for many months, and are interesting and pretty for the winter decoration of rooms.

Christmas Decorations

Victorian Christmas decorations seem particularly appropriate to the holiday, perhaps because so many of us were brought up on Dickens' *Christmas Carol*. The gaily trimmed Christmas tree, long a Germanic tradition, had been introduced in England by Queen Caroline; but it remained for Victoria's beloved Prince Albert to popularize it. So that today, an English Christmas without one would of course be unthinkable. Here are decorations for a festive house and for a glorious tree.

Decorating the House

These hints will make it an easy task to adorn the house for Christmas; but half the pleasure consists in inventing new devices, and giving scope to one's taste and ingenuity, new ideas springing up and developing themselves as the occasion arises, till the worker finds delight in the work, and is thus best rewarded for the toil.

Fig. 1 is a bordering for the cornice of a hall or large room, and is made of laurel leaves and rosettes of colored paper or immortelles or straw flowers.

Fig. 2 is a monogram signifying Christmas, and is very pretty made of cardboard and covered with leaves and berries, or moss, glued on another piece of cardboard, and edged with three different shades of immortelles. The outside row of star-points is made with ferns.

In Fig. 3 the trefoil is made of holly leaves, and the border of laurel.

In Fig. 4 will be found a bold and effective device for a large space, as, for example, to hang on the end wall of an entrance-hall

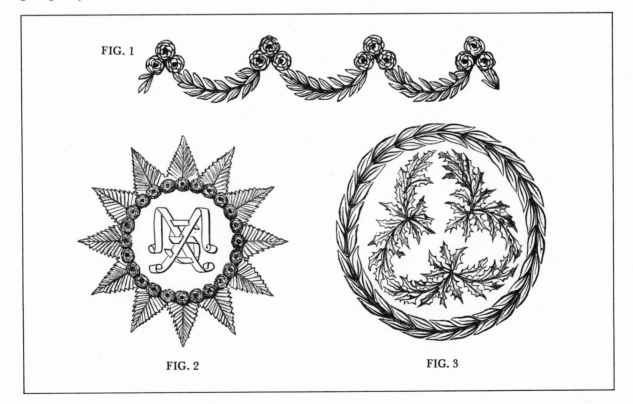

FIG. 1

FIG. 2

FIG. 3

FIG. 4

or landing. The cross-pieces are stout sticks, the size of which must be regulated by the space intended to be filled; and it will be found advisable to join them in the center by a cross joint [that is, each branch half cut away where they join] *, otherwise they will be very awkward to manage. They can then be wreathed with holly and mistletoe, as shown in the figure. The legend surrounding them is made of letters in gilt paper, pasted on to colored cardboard, and the figure of the robin is cut out in cardboard and painted.*

Decorating the Tree

CORNUCOPIAS

To make a simple paper cornucopia as shown in Fig. 5, cut a piece of fairly heavy fancy paper the shape of Fig. 7 along the solid lines. Cut out a piece of lightweight paper for lining, using the inner broken lines as a guide. Cut two pieces of narrow ribbon or cord 9" long and glue an end of each on the wrong side of the fancy paper where the stars are marked. Now glue the lining in place on top of the ribbon. Roll into a cone shape with an overlap of about ½" at point A to none at B, and glue. Trim the top edge, both inside and out with paper braid or ribbon and sew a tassel to the bottom.

To make fabric-covered cornucopias, cut lightweight cardboard by the solid line in Fig. 7 and the fabric by the outer broken lines. Fold the fabric tightly over the card-

board and glue the excess on the wrong side. Glue in the ribbons and lining as before. Butt the edges together from A to B and sew with tiny, concealed stitches. Trimmings may be either sewn or glued in place. If you use glue, it is wise to use special fabric glue to prevent staining. This is sold in craft stores.

To make a bag top as shown in Fig. 6, for either a paper or fabric cornucopia, cut a piece of lightweight silk by the pattern, Fig. 8. Clip the silk to the dot on the fold line; press under at the dotted hem lines. Fold it over again at the fold line and press to form a casing, and sew in place with small stitches. Run a ribbon or cord through the casing. Seam the bag together, matching the notches. Gather along the gathering line and adjust to the size of the cone top. Glue or sew in place on the outside rim of the cornucopia. Cover the join with lace, ribbon, or gold-paper braid. Cornucopias with bag tops can be hung from the ribbon tying the bag, so they need not have any other hangers.

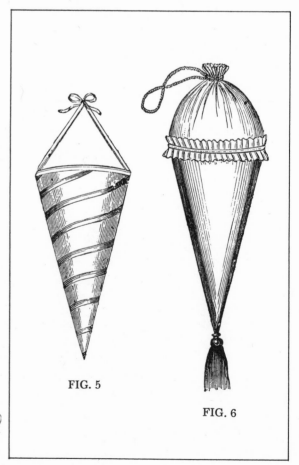

FIG. 5

FIG. 6

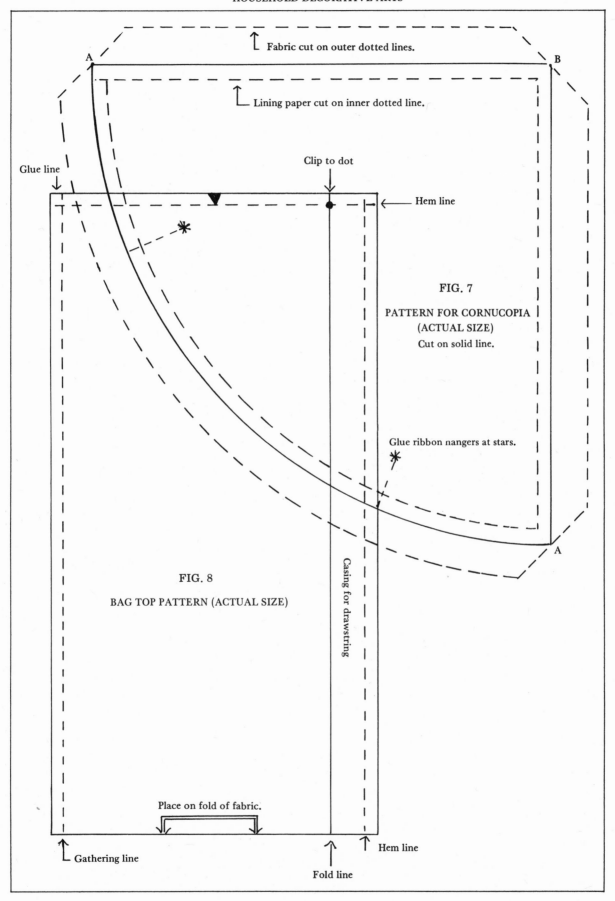

Fabric cut on outer dotted lines.

Lining paper cut on inner dotted line.

A

B

Glue line

Clip to dot

Hem line

FIG. 7

PATTERN FOR CORNUCOPIA
(ACTUAL SIZE)
Cut on solid line.

Glue ribbon nangers at stars.

A

Casing for drawstring

FIG. 8

BAG TOP PATTERN (ACTUAL SIZE)

Place on fold of fabric.

Gathering line

Fold line

Hem line

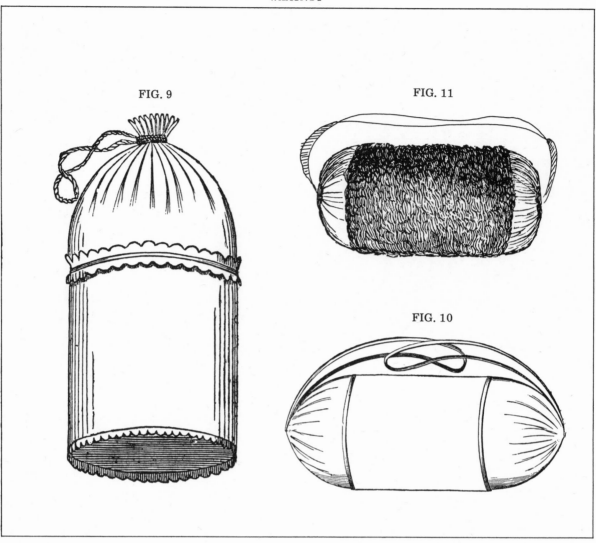

FIG. 9

FIG. 11

FIG. 10

SUGAR-PLUM CASES

To make sugar-plum cases as in Fig. 9, cut pieces of lightweight cardboard to the size of Figs. 14 and 15 (see page 180) along the solid lines. Cut fabric coverings for both along the broken lines. Clip the fabric in, almost to the cardboard around the curve of the circle. Glue the edges and proceed as with the cornucopias with bag tops, Fig. 8.

MUFFS

Two styles of muffs, Figs. 10 and 11, are made from the same pattern Fig. 14. Make the circle of lightweight cardboard by gluing the tab inside. Make two bag tops as in the cornucopia directions. For Fig. 11, the bags are made narrower and elastic run through the casing. Glue on a ribbon hanger. Glue the bags to the outside rims of the circle. Cut

the fabric the size of Fig. 14 along the broken lines. Turn the edges in all around, press and glue in place over the gathered edges of the bags. Trim as desired.

DRUMS

Make the drum of colored poster board cut to the size of Fig. 14 along the solid lines. Form into a ring and glue the tab inside. Decorate as shown in Fig. 12 with ribbon or gold paper. Glue a ribbon hanger to the inside. Cut the top and bottom of heavy white paper, to the pattern of Fig. 16. Score along the broken lines with a razor knife and turn the tabs down. Apply glue to the tabs on one and insert into the drum at the bottom. Glue two small loops of ribbon to the top for handles. Fill the drum with sweetmeats and insert the lid without gluing.

LUCKY SHOES

To make lucky shoes as in Fig. 13, cut a piece of stiff cardboard to the shape of Fig. 17, and a piece of lightweight cardboard to the shape of Fig. 18 along the solid lines. Cut some lightweight silk the size of Fig. 17 along the broken lines and some bright-colored velvet for Fig. 18. Clip the fabric all around and glue it over the cardboard. Butt the heel edges together matching the A's and B's and sew with tiny stitches. Now carefully sew on the sole. Make a bag top as in Fig. 8 and glue it to the inside top edge of the shoe or sew it to the outside edge and cover the raw edges with braid or lace.

BONBON BOXES

To make these charming little boxes, cut some lightweight poster board in a pretty color by the pattern in Fig 19. Lightly score with a razor knife along the broken lines. Fold and glue the tabs to form the box. Glue a ribbon hanger on each side and trim top and bottom with gold-paper borders or ribbon. Decorate each side and the top with cutout pictures or Christmas seals. See page 182.

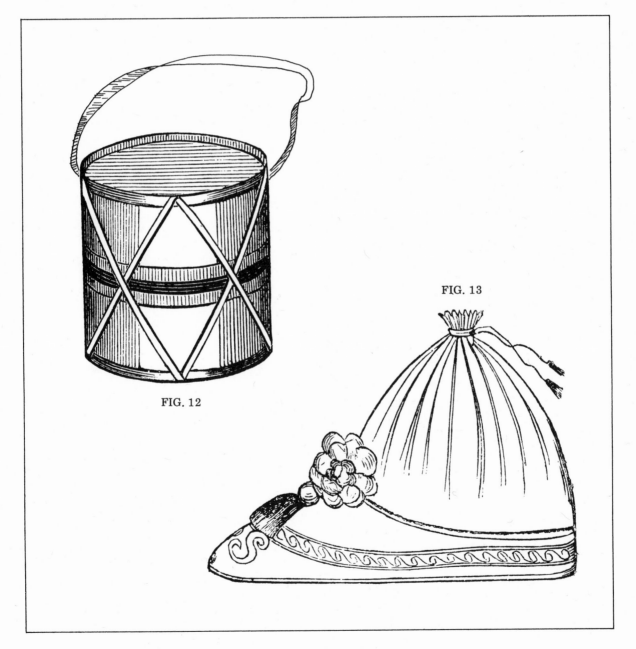

FIG. 13

FIG. 12

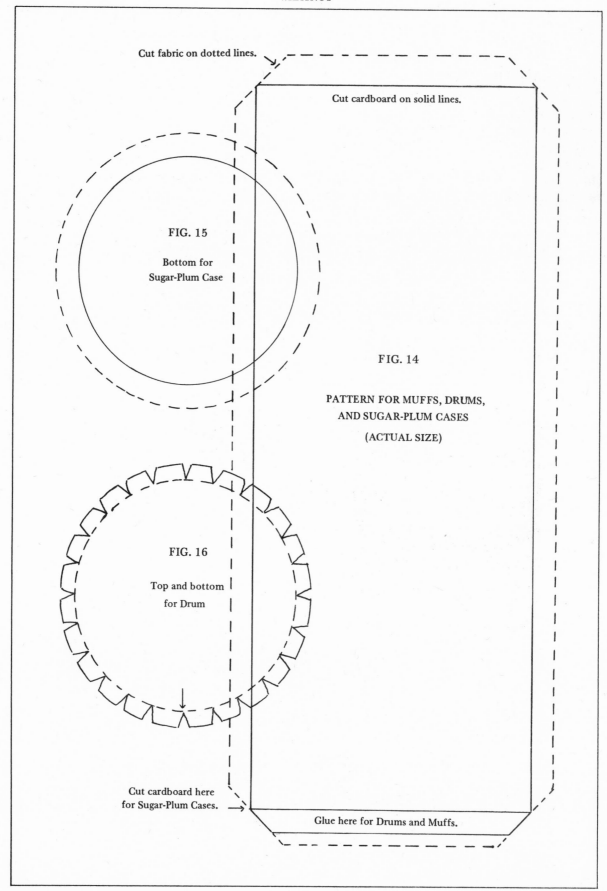

Cut fabric on dotted lines.

Cut cardboard on solid lines.

FIG. 15

Bottom for
Sugar-Plum Case

FIG. 14

PATTERN FOR MUFFS, DRUMS,
AND SUGAR-PLUM CASES

(ACTUAL SIZE)

FIG. 16

Top and bottom
for Drum

Cut cardboard here
for Sugar-Plum Cases.

Glue here for Drums and Muffs.

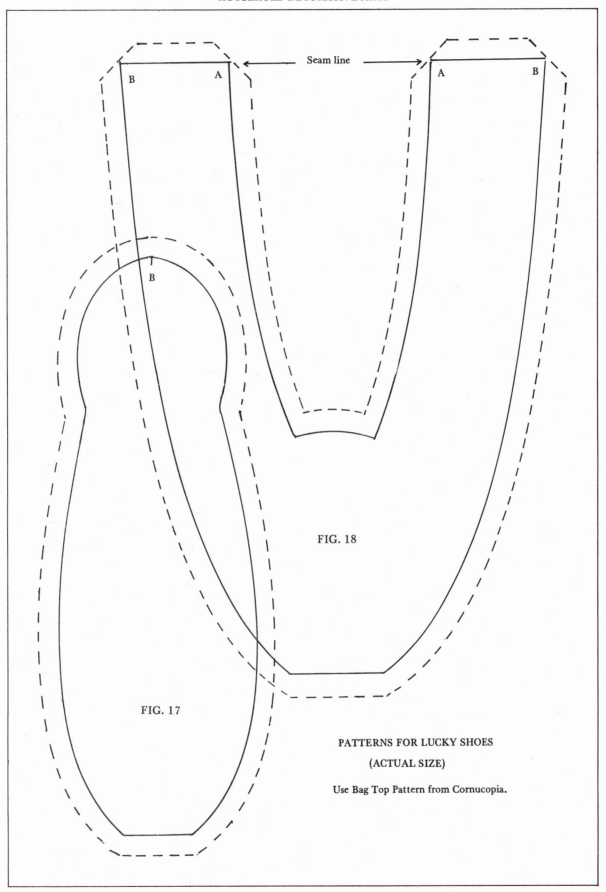

Seam line

B A   A B

FIG. 18

B

FIG. 17

PATTERNS FOR LUCKY SHOES

(ACTUAL SIZE)

Use Bag Top Pattern from Cornucopia.

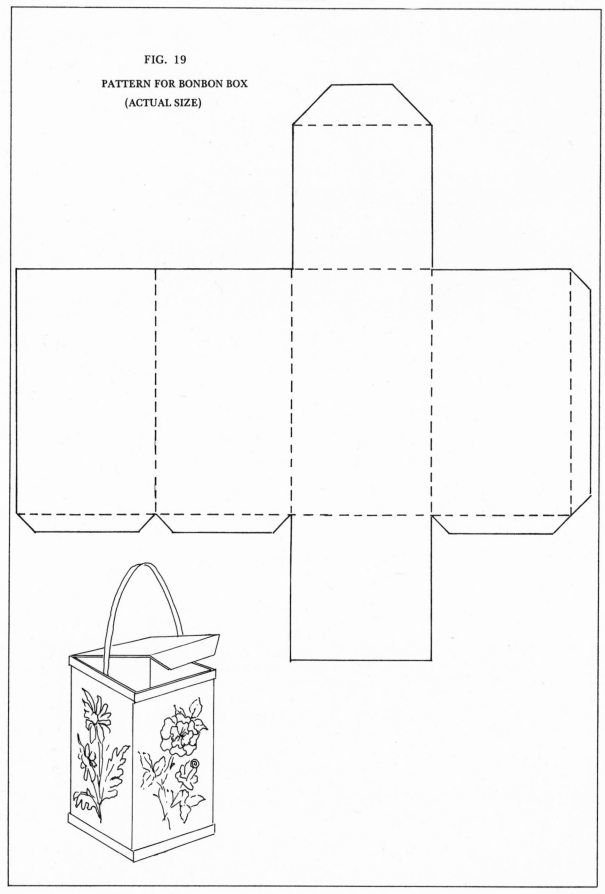

FIG. 19

PATTERN FOR BONBON BOX
(ACTUAL SIZE)

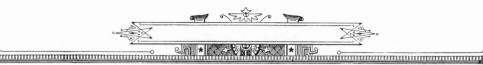

PART THREE

IN THE GARDEN

Rockwork and Grottoes

An Aeolian Harp

Rustic Garden Furniture

Flower Containers

Summer Houses

Fern Cases

Floral Ornaments for Windows and Back Yards

Tame Pigeons and Doves

Sun Dials

Introduction

THE DEEP APPRECIATION the English have for their lovely countryside has always expressed itself in garden design of a high order.
This preoccupation is nowhere so amusingly and accurately
described as in Jane Austen's *Mansfield Park*, where the entire cast
of characters set out to advise Mr. Rushworth on how to improve
his grounds. Such eighteenth-century great estate gardens as
Mr. Rushworth's, with their plantation walks, mazes, Greek
temples, and "Gothic ruins," were an inspiration to the middle-class Victorian in designing the more modest grounds of his country house or
suburban villa. These same features, reduced in scale, were translated into
informal, rustic designs that could be executed by the amateur carpenter. In
short, the do-it-yourself school of landscape design makes its appearance in
the pages of Cassell's.

We have, up to this point, probably given the impression that Cassell
addressed himself almost exclusively to the pursuits of ladies, but this is
not so. Half of the material in the *Household Guide* deals with the concerns of
the Victorian gentleman and of his gardener, his tenant farmer, and his

handyman. (Cassell covers such varied topics as drunken grooms, bell hanging, fire alarums, and carriage maintenance.) We found that many of his garden projects could still be used with charming effect today—the vine displays, for example, are suitable for city yards, and the many types of decorative planters would be attractive almost anywhere.

Perhaps you will never aspire to a grotto, but why not while away a sunny afternoon at the bottom of your garden in a rustic summer house.

Rockwork and Grottoes

Oh, for a balmy afternoon, a copy of *Wuthering Heights,* a rustic seat in a Gothic hermitage, and a tame owl!

Rock-work may often be made of considerable use, especially in town or suburban gardens, where space is necessarily limited; since by means of it the apparent extent may be increased, and paths, separated by judicious arrangements of this nature, may be brought close together without their proximity being observed; not to speak of its value in giving those picturesque forms and broken lines so pleasing to the eye, or in affording proper habitations to ferns and other beautiful kinds of vegetation. And some remarks on the principles which constitute sound taste in this matter seem especially needed, since there are few subjects upon which more mistaken views are generally held, or in which bad taste is so rampant, as in what is known by the name of "rock-work." In some places we see a heterogeneous mixture of pebbles, flints, and shells, scattered loosely over a mound of earth. This may afford a place for growing certain descriptions of plants, and so far be useful, but it has no claim to be considered rock-work, and in itself, to a cultivated eye and thoughtful mind, its appearance will be anything but pleasing.

Far worse than this are the vulgarities we sometimes see perpetrated; plaster-casts (generally broken), oyster-shells and even the remains of bottles and tea cups, are, after their legitimate work is accomplished, made to do service as "decorations of the rockery." These things call up associations the very reverse of those which it is the object of gardening and garden decoration to arouse. The real motive of ornamental gardening is to call back the mind, from the dull lowering influences of artificial life, to the beauty and purity

of Nature; and therefore those things which have an opposite tendency are wholly to be condemned.

Some few years ago we saw a rockery, in the bottom of which were dens, grated in the front, and stocked with miniature wild beasts in plaster! This was, of course, an evidence of taste on the part of the proprietor; but he must have possessed, as Beau Brummel once said of George IV, "a great deal of taste — and all of it bad."

Rock-work produces good effects, and is in true taste only when it is in harmony with the principles upon which Nature constructs her rocks. Hence the stratified arrangement of natural rocks, more or less inclining to the horizontal, should be followed in the layers of stones used in their artificial representatives, varied, as they are in Nature by frequent irregularities, which should have the appearance of resulting from natural causes, such as the giving away of subsoils, or the displacement by roots of trees. The larger the masses of stone and the more picturesque their shapes, the better will be their effect.

In some quarries are to be found crystalised masses of carbonate or quartz, having a very beautiful appearance. These should not be used for outside purposes, for they will not harmonize with surrounding objects, and are not in accordance with the laws of Nature, since crystal can only be formed where filtration takes place; but if a cavern is made in the rockery, these stones are admirably adapted for lining it, and will appear in good taste.

Pebbles and shells will not look well forming part of the rock-work itself; but if its base be washed by water they will make an appropriate border; and pebbles strewn in the course of an artificial stream will have a pleasing effect.

Between rocks and water there is a natural harmony. If, therefore, it be possible to arrange a pond at the base of the rock-work, into which some of its jutting points may protrude, it should always be done. . . .

In our illustration (Fig. 1) we give an example, in which a miniature sheet of water is enclosed between the irregular horns of a crescent of rock. The supply pipe by which the former is fed is brought into the rock-work near the top and miniature cascades are thus formed.

On the whole a rockery should have a slope of 45 degrees, which will exhibit plants to the best advantage, and be more in character with ordinary English scenery. At the back of the rockery, which will probably be only intended to be seen at a short distance, a more abrupt rise may be indulged in, which may be useful as affording shelter to ferns and other plants delighting in the shade.

A good feature may be made by the introduction of a cavern, larger or smaller size according to circumstances; ivy may be trained to droop over its entrance, and if it be on a sufficiently large scale to contain one or more seats, it will afford a deliciously cool retreat in summer; if too small for this purpose, it is of all others the place to keep a tame owl.

In the construction of caverns, either in artificial or in the natural rock, the necessity for avoiding all trace of human labor does not hold good, since a cavern, if intended for a retreat, becomes a thing of use as well as of ornament, and good taste demands that it should be rendered commodious as well as pleasing to the eye. We are, moreover, accustomed to associate caves with the idea of their having served as habitations for man in a rude state of society, and some adaptation, therefore, of their interior to human wants rather increases than diminishes the picturesque and romantic pleasure they arouse; but, for the same reason, nothing that is connected with modern life ought to find a place in them and such furniture as they contain should be of a rude and primitive kind. In our illustration, Fig. 3, we have shown a cavern, in which the table is formed of the root of a tree.

If a person should be fortunate enough to possess a garden in an old stone quarry, or on which a natural cliff abuts, he will have an excellent opportunity for excavating a hermitage, which is a thing not only pleasing in itself, but interesting from its associations with poetry and romance. In our illustration (Fig. 2) we have shown such a one, which has been fitted with a Gothic window and doorway; and to those contemplating a work of this kind it may afford useful suggestions. . . .

FIG. 1

FIG. 2

FIG. 3

An Aeolian Harp

This is one of the projects that we did not attempt. The drawing is our interpretation of the directions given, so we cannot be positive that it is completely accurate. But the Aeolian harp is such a delightful idea that it seems to us someone else is sure to want to experiment with it.

An instrument of the kind about to be described seems to be of very ancient origin, but was re-introduced during the last century. The Aeolian Harp produces a very pleasing, melodious sound, especially in the open air, and is not difficult to construct.

A long narrow box, the length of the window, or the position in which it is to be placed, is the first requisite; it must be made of deal [pine], four inches deep and five in width. At the extremities of the top, glue two pieces of oak about half an inch high and a quarter of an inch thick, for bridges to which the strings are to be fixed; within the box, at each end, glue two pieces of beech-wood, about an inch square and the width of the box. Into one of the bridges fix seven pegs, such as are used for piano strings; into the other bridge fasten the same number of small brass pins; and to these pins fix one end of the strings, made of small catgut, and twist the other end of the strings round the pegs; then tune them in unison. Place over the top of the strings a thin board, supported by four pegs, and about three inches from the sounding board, to procure a free passage for the wind. The harp should be exposed to the wind at a partly open window; to increase the draught of air, the door, or an opposite window in the room, should be open. The strings in a current of air sound in unison, and with increasing or decreasing force of the current, the melody changes into pleasing, soft, low sounds and diatonic scales, which unite and occasionally form very delightful

musical tones. If the harp can be placed in a suitable position, so as to receive a sufficient draught of air, in a grotto, or romantically situated arbor, or hidden in some shady nook near a waterfall, the effect of its sweet sounds is very charming.

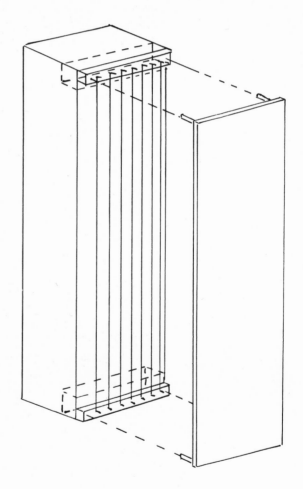

Rustic Garden Furniture

Many pretty kinds of rustic garden seats and tables may be constructed by the amateur workman; however much depends on his taste and ingenuity. The best results may be obtained when the branches used retain their natural outlines. To effect this is a matter of some difficulty; but perseverence and patience will be sure to succeed.

It will at once occur to the ingenious reader that there are many ways in which these ideas may be carried out. In fact, working with such varied forms as the branches of trees. . . it is well nigh impossible to produce two articles exactly alike; and this alone is sufficient to show how infinitely superior in appearance and artistic natural effect, such garden furniture will be when compared with the ordinary angular and incongruous-looking combinations of right-lines and square surfaces, which are too frequently met with where such things are most certainly out of place.

To construct a rustic seat with back and elbows is a rather difficult operation; but, beside the extra comfort of such a seat, its very pretty appearance will quite repay the trouble involved. See Fig. 1.

A very pretty rustic table may be made out of the stump of a small uprooted tree, if the roots have not been cut off too near the trunk. See Fig. 2. If a section of a larger tree can be obtained, of the size required for the top, and about three inches in thickness, and having the bark on round the edges, it may be nailed to the top, and the table will be complete.

In Fig. 3 is shown a seat, intended to go half round the base of a tree standing at the edge of a lawn, backed by a hedge or shrubbery.

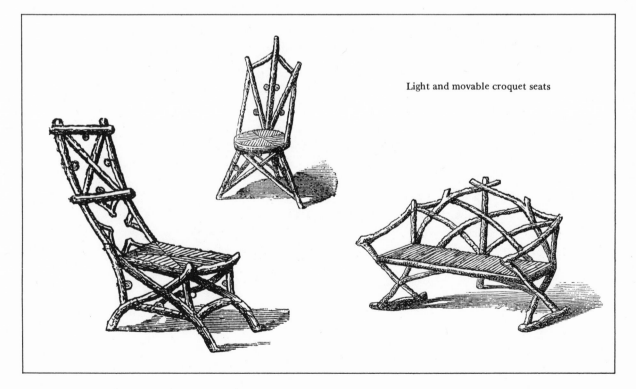

Light and movable croquet seats

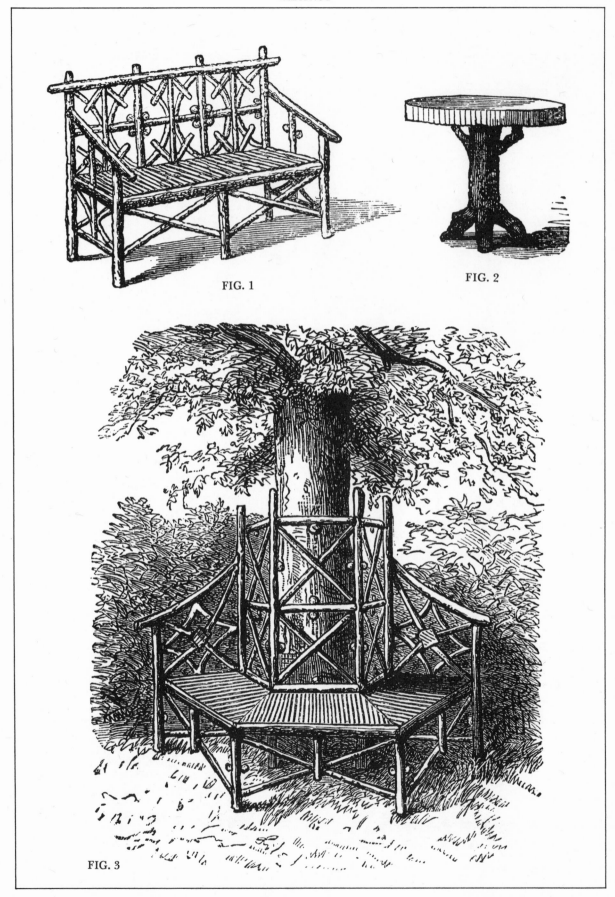

FIG. 1

FIG. 2

FIG. 3

A doll-size rustic settee, perfect for a picnic under a peony.

Rustic Settee for a Doll

Cassell's illustrations show just some of the charming pieces that can be made with natural branches. We selected the settee in Fig. 1 to reproduce and reduced the scale to accommodate a Victorian pennywood doll.

You will need:

Dry branches (we used apple prunings because the gnarled forms and many curved spurs lent themselves to the design)
Pruning shears
Utility razor knife
Vise
Drill
Brads
Glue

The size of the piece will depend on what you intend to use it for. Doll-house furniture is usually scaled 1" to 1' life size. A full-size piece would measure about 60" long, 30" deep, 17" seat height, and 32" back height. If you are making it for a larger doll, use a heel to knee measurement for seat height and double it for back height. Use a back of the knee to buttocks measurement for the depth of the seat, and make it wide enough for two dolls to sit comfortably with a picnic basket between them.

Following the drawing, Fig. 4, cut the branches to the correct lengths with pruning shears. Use heavier pieces for the legs and seat frames; rungs and decorative back pieces may be smaller in diameter. Be sure to cut

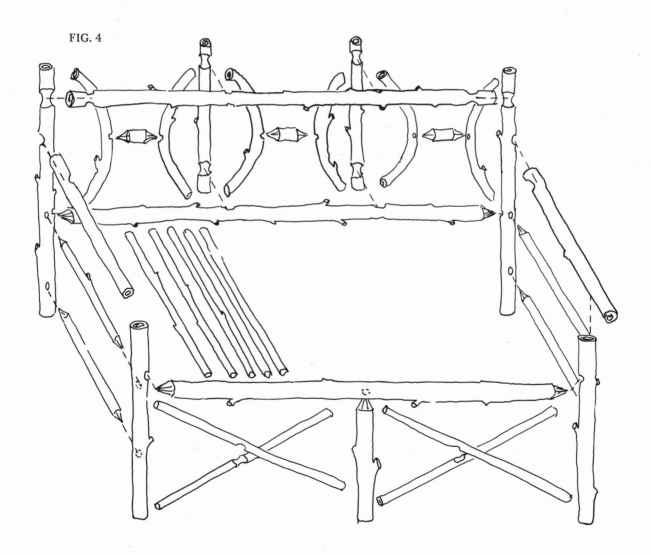

FIG. 4

the leg bottoms squarely across, so that they stand firmly.

Lay the parts for the back and front out flat on the table. With the razor knife, whittle the seat-frame pieces to a point at each end. Carefully measure and mark on the legs where the seat frames and rungs belong. Holding the leg steady in a vise, drill holes large enough to receive the pointed ends of the frames and rungs. Apply glue to all points and assemble. These are known as mortice and tenon joints and in full-scale furniture would be cut as in Fig. 5.

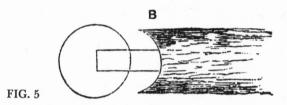

FIG. 5

Mark the places where the horizontal back piece and the uprights intersect and halve both pieces with the razor knife so that they fit into each other and are level. Fig. 6 shows a branch that has been halved. Glue the pieces of wood in place.

FIG. 6

Drill holes in the six curved back pieces; glue and insert the three pointed separators. Glue the assembled pieces between the back uprights. Halve and glue the crisscrossed rungs and glue them between the front legs. Glue and insert the side frames and rungs. Halve and glue the arms into the back and nail them with tiny brads to the top of the front legs.

The seat surface is made of straight sticks of uniform size, cut long enough to rest firmly on the front and back seat frame. Glue in place.

If you were constructing full-scale furniture, all the pieces not morticed and tenoned would be bolted or screwed together.

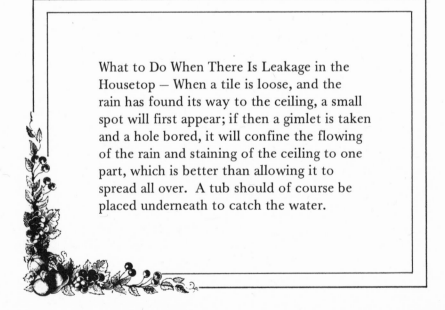

What to Do When There Is Leakage in the Housetop — When a tile is loose, and the rain has found its way to the ceiling, a small spot will first appear; if then a gimlet is taken and a hole bored, it will confine the flowing of the rain and staining of the ceiling to one part, which is better than allowing it to spread all over. A tub should of course be placed underneath to catch the water.

Flower Containers

The most splendid of Mr. Cassell's several ideas for flower containers is this elaborate column under an enormous glass shade which was meant to be constructed of Watsonian Patent Fern Bricks. The bricks were made, primarily, to be built into the walls of conservatories and were fitted with removable shell-shaped planters. One wonders if anyone ever actually assembled one of these marvelous giant terrariums or if it was simply a fanciful idea, dreamed up in a gray London office.

Cassell's other ideas are more practical, and even though they are less fantastic, some produce results that are quite handsome.

Rustic Hanging Baskets

Elegant hanging baskets for windows or greenhouses can be made at home.

Branches of a tree about three inches wide, even, smooth and equal, are wanted; and the silver bark [such as birch] *looks especially well.*

There are four pieces to every side, and two for the bottom which should be as uniform as possible. Drill holes in all of them about an inch from the end.

String four stout but very slender wires through the holes in two of the branches and secure them well. Take a square of wood and drill holes in all four corners and pass the wires through them. See Fig. 1. Then string the other logs on the wires, four to each side as shown in Fig. 2. Unite the wires at the top. Fill the sides of the basket, between the logs, profusely with moss and also the top when the flower-pot is inside.

Fig. 3 represents a basket made of rough pieces of rustic wood joined together in another manner.

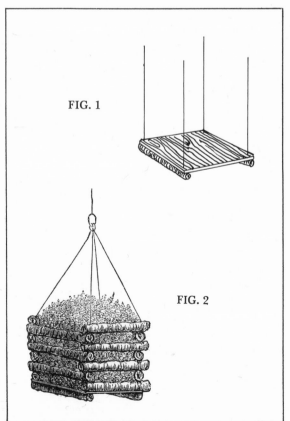

FIG. 1

FIG. 2

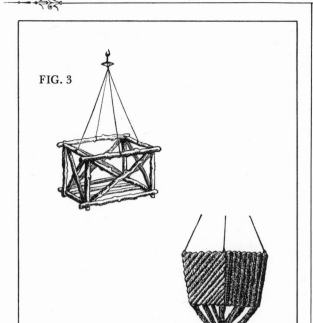

FIG. 3

FIG. 4

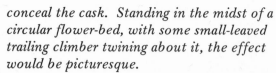
conceal the cask. *Standing in the midst of a circular flower-bed, with some small-leaved trailing climber twining about it, the effect would be picturesque.*

An even more picturesque effect would be obtained by using sections of a hollow tree, having rugged, fantastic outlines ranged about the base of such a stand, with flowers growing in the eccentric holes and hollows.

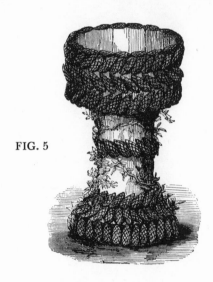

FIG. 5

Fancy Work with Acorns

Acorns may be made the medium of holding ferns in a variety of pretty ways, either in a room or, still better, in a greenhouse, or small window garden, opening, perhaps, out of a back parlor or drawing room. The acorns are soft when new, and a hole may readily be made by slipping through them a large upholstery needle. Thread them on wire, a large, round-cut white glass bead between every one. The wire [24 guage galvanized] *is bought by the piece, in a coil.*

Fig. 6 is an urn of acorns. Make first the ring for the top and a ring for the bottom, strung with acorns. Crook the top of the wire, and hook it to the ring for the top between the acorns, pinching it close, and not showing the join. Thread it with acorns till it is long enough to form the outline of the vase which shows at A in Fig. 6, to cross at the narrow part, to form the swell of the base, B, and hook to the lower ring. The wire is then cut off. The other side is made in the same way,

For large out-of-door [hanging] *baskets suitable for summer-houses, the best we have seen were made of small butter-firkins decorated as we shall describe.* [We haven't seen a butter-firkin in years and would suggest using a common redwood planter as a base.] *In order to decorate this, split branches may be used, in some cases placed at right angles to the top, in others obliquely, as in Fig. 4. The bottom of the basket may be ornamented by placing a group of crooked branches, as shown in the same Figure, and the effect is very rustic and pretty. Holes must be bored in the upper part for the wires, and a number of small holes bored in the bottom to allow of the escape of water.*

Plant Stand

Fig. 5 is a sketch of a rustic basket or vase, for which we are indebted to the kindness of a correspondent. It was formed of an old cask sawn in two, and placed upon a pedestal formed of the trunk of an old tree, having the bark unremoved. The bottom of the trunk was fastened to a heavy block of wood. The decorations were pine cones, with moss pushed into the spaces between them so as to

This hanging basket made of acorns can hold a flower pot or a container made of chicken wire covered with sphagnum moss and filled with planting mix.

and the two crossed each by another piece diagonally. If the urn is large, there may be two of these on each side, making six equal sides to the urn, instead of four.

Where they cross at the narrow part of the base, bind them well together with fine wool, or strong thread. Do not let this binding show. Bend the six pieces into a good shape.

Join [a piece of] wire to one of them, and carry a ring [of acorns and beads] round the widest part of the urn at C, joining it with wire to every part where it crosses.

Then put on the upper vandykes [the V shapes connecting the horizontal rows on Fig. 6], and lastly the lower ones, joining them as before.

The urn handles are rings of acorns, and may be attached last, or made in one with the large ring at C by twisting the wire. There should only be two of them. The number of acorns should be equal in relative parts, and in the rings between the side pieces the wires should be well closed.

Fill the urn with moss, and plant with ferns. The glass beads glisten out of the moss and the brown acorns like so many dew drops.

Fig. 7 is an acorn hanging basket. It is made precisely in the same manner, and may be suspended by a metal chain. Such baskets should be filled with moss and ferns, red-leafe begonias, ice plants, and red-leafed American nettles mixed in them.

We liked the look of acorns with their caps on so we made a hanging basket without the dew drops. Perhaps green acorns are as easy to run through with a heavy needle as Cassell says, but ripe glossy brown ones need special treatment. First, separate the acorns and caps. Then bore holes in the cap centers with a fine bit in a hand drill. To make lengthwise holes in the acorns, use a hammer and long thin nail. If the acorns prove too slippery, try this: Drill a hole in a block of wood — the hole should be a little wider than the acorn, and almost as deep as the acorn is long — and drop the acorn in point down. Then go at it with hammer and nail.

Horse chestnuts will make similar baskets, not forgetting the alternate bead, which gives much lightness and finish. An amber colored bead in place of a white one accords well with the chestnuts.

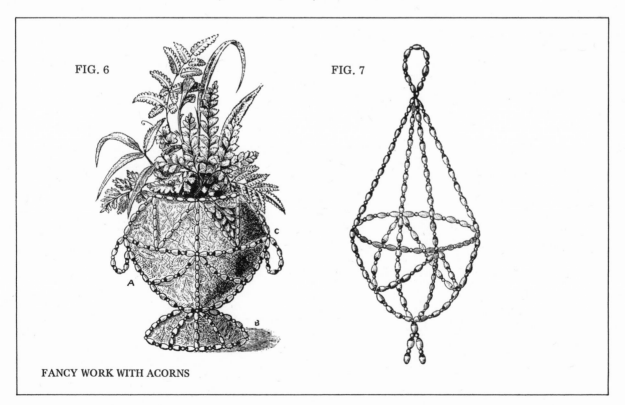

FIG. 6

FIG. 7

FANCY WORK WITH ACORNS

Summer Houses

These charming little gazebos are, perhaps, a come-down from the Greek temples and pagodas of the previous century, but they certainly were and are practicable for the amateur builder. We may disagree with Cassell's opinions on pagodas, but we cannot help but concur that his designs would be a great improvement over the standard park structures of today. Happily, there seems to be a trend back to lighthearted garden houses, at least in home gardens.

Since there are many modern books of instruction on building techniques and anyone who plans to build one of these structures will probably know fairly well what he or she is doing, we have eliminated Cassell's construction details and included only his general descriptions and philosophizings on the subject.

A summer-house, to be as pleasurable and useful an addition to the garden as it should be, must be situated in an attractive and sheltered location.

It sometimes happens that an otherwise picturesque garden is marred in effect by the presence of an ugly piece of wall, or an out-building. In this case a summer-house, erected so as to shut out a view of the offensive object, will not only be useful, but conduce to the pleasant effect which the garden ought to produce upon the mind. Nothing of this sort, however, is effected by the erection of such ungainly structures as we frequently meet with even in our parks, which ought to be models in this respect. A Chinese pagoda is most certainly as much out of place in an English landscape as anything can well be; yet, in two, at least, of our metropolitan parks these monstrosities are to be met with. No less out of keeping are the square boxes, fitted with taproom tables, of which the Londoners seem so fond, and which look like a compromise between the cuddy-houses, usually found upon the decks of sea-going ships, and gigantic hen-roosts. We will endeavor to show how summer-houses may be constructed so as to avoid these common defects, and be made to add to the rustic effect and beauty of the gardens in which they are erected.

A sure and certain method of making a building ugly, is to make the roof flat. The

FIG. 1

DESIGNS FOR LATTICEWORK

best and most effective method is to make the roof "hipped" — that is, so that it slopes from the center point down to all the sides. The inclination should be bold and well marked, both for the purpose of throwing the water off quickly and for the sake of effective appearance.

The apex of the roof may be ornamented according to taste, and the only thing which need here be said, may be in the shape of a caution, to avoid the ordinary conventional weathercock, which is most certainly out of place on the top of such a structure. See Fig. 1.

FIG. 2

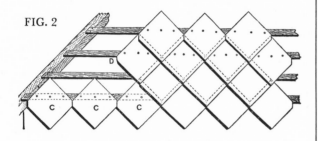

In places where timber with the bark on is not easily available, and tiles are expensive, a very neat summer-house may be made with laths and having a shingled roof as shown. See Fig. 2.

FIG. 3

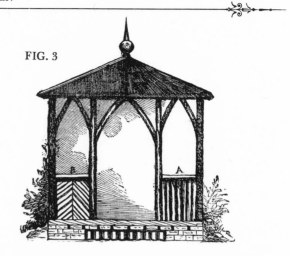

It is rarely required that the whole of the space between the roof and the floor will need to be left open, except in that portion used as the entrance. The remaining spaces will therefore require filling up. A very good plan is to cut a piece of round timber to fit between the uprights as shown in Fig. 3. This will form a sort of sill.

The remaining space may then be filled with branches, either squarely, as at A, Fig. 3, or diagonally as at B, as may be preferred. Some care will be required in fitting, in order not to injure the bark of the wood, which should be preserved as far as possible.

FIG. 4

FIG. 5

The square junction of the uprights and the lintel supporting the roof should be broken up by means of crooked or curved branches cut to fit both parts, and nailed to them, so as to form a sort of rustic arch over all the openings, of course selecting for use only such pieces as have graceful curves, and are of picturesque outline.

It should always be remembered, that the more varied forms are far more elegant and ornamental; and that the extra trouble involved will be amply repaid when the work is completed.

In the two summer-houses, Figs. 4 and 5 [see page 205], the uprights and other main timbers are formed of young fir. The roofs are covered with a good coating of ordinary thatch, not less than a foot in thickness. This open work looks complicated, but as it is for the most part simply nailed together, it may be made very quickly.

The backs of both summer-houses are formed by nailing boards outside the uprights. . . and are covered within with split branch-work arranged in patterns as indicated in the pictures. In both, the seats are made in the same manner. As bare thatch is unsightly, the spaces between the rafters may be filled with heather, if it can be obtained, if not, with moss, but the use of the latter has this attendant evil — in springtine it forms a source of overpowering temptation to the birds, who look upon it as specially adapted to their own architectural requirements, and appropriate it in the most unscrupulous manner, much to the disadvantage of the human race to which it properly belongs.

To Restore Plants Apparently Killed by Frost — When plants in pots, such as geraniums, are found to be frozen, they should never be placed near the fire, but should at once be plunged in a bucket of cold water, or pumped upon, but the former process is by far to be preferred, as being less likely to break the leaves, which will be rendered extremely brittle by frost. When thawed by the water, they should be placed in a room sufficiently warm to preclude the possibility of their again freezing, but at a distance from the fire. Plants that have been frozen often appear to be dead, when such is not really the case, and when their vitality is merely at low ebb; they may, under such circumstances, be stimulated, and again brought into vigorous health by moistening them with water in which guano has been dissolved.

Fern Cases

Within the last few years the exquisitely beautiful plants known as ferns have become quite household favorites; so much so, in fact, that a drawing room without its one or more fern cases would now be considered scarcely furnished. We show fern cases of a rustic pattern through which the beautiful forms of the plants may be observed, in lieu of the ordinary square and inelegant lines in which they are usually enclosed.

We liked the designs for these charming miniature conservatories but found that the construction details were far beyond the scope of our carpentry skills. After trying to saw one gnarled branch down its entire length, as Cassell directs, we ended up with fifteen splintered segments and gave up in despair. We then turned our minds to a different approach, and this method, while not authentic in detail, produces the desired effect.

A FERN CASE

Hexagonal Rustic Fern Case

You will need:

Plexiglas, 30" by 36", 1/8" thick
Acrylic plastic cement, solvent type
Needle-end solvent applicator
Plexiglas cutting tool, or sabre saw
Instant mold-making compound
Casting plaster
Oil paints
Waterproof glue
Small tree branches
Acorns or small pine cones
Galvanized wire, 18 gauge
Two cake pans, about 12" by 8"
Plywood, 18" square of ½" thick
Clear acrylic spray finish
Masking tape
Razor knife
Sandpaper
Enamel paint, dark brown or black
Felt

Leave the protective paper on the Plexiglas and measure out on it six rectangles and six triangles as shown in Fig. 1.

On a plain piece of paper draw a base plan of the case as shown in Fig. 2.

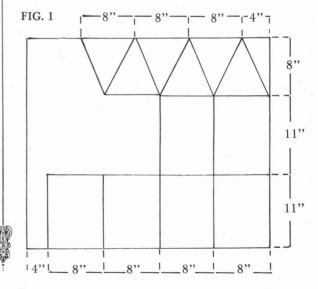

FIG. 1

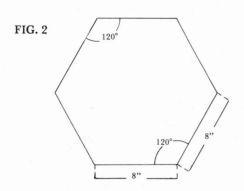

FIG. 2

120°

120°   8"

8"

Cut the Plexiglas carefully with a special cutting tool or with a sabre saw. Detailed cutting instructions are provided at stores selling Plexiglas and some stores will cut it for you. Sand the edges and remove the protective paper.

Assemble the entire case on the base plan, and tape the pieces firmly together with masking tape. See Fig. 3. Apply the solvent-type cement to all the joins, taking care that it does not run down the Plexiglas. Allow it to dry thoroughly before removing the tape.

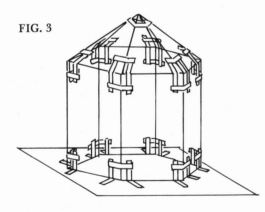

FIG. 3

Cut branches of fairly smooth-barked wood to correspond with the sizes and shapes shown in Fig. 4 (see page 211).

Mix enough mold-making compound to fill one cake pan to the depth of 1". Quickly place the branch A in the wet compound and press it in until it is slightly more than half covered. Place branches B, C, and D next, leaving *a good inch* between all the branches and making sure that they are embedded slightly more than halfway into the compound. Add several acorns of varying sizes as in Fig. 5.

When the mold is quite firm, carefully remove the branches making sure you do not tear the mold.

Prepare a second pan of mold-making compound in the same manner, and again embed branch A, only this time *turn it over* so that the curved side branch projects in the reverse direction. Remold branches B, C, and D and some acorns as before. When the second mold is firm, remove the branches and acorns. Don't throw them away because you may need them again. We found that our molds started to deteriorate after the fourth casting and had to be remade.

Cut a piece of wire the length of each of the four branches and one for the side branch on A so that it extends an inch or so down the main stem of A. The acorns will not need these wire reinforcements. Lay a wire in each mold, making sure that the wire does not protrude above the surface of the mold.

Measure a cup of water into a coffee can or bowl and add plaster of paris a little at a time, mixing vigorously until it is the consistency of heavy cream. Pour this mixture into each mold until it fills completely and the plaster of paris is just level with the top of the mold. Slight overflows can be trimmed off later. You must work quickly once the plaster of paris is mixed as it sets up very quickly.

When your molds are full, set them aside to dry and clean your mixing tools before the plaster hardens on them. A plastic bucket filled with water is convenient for cleaning up. Don't wash up in the sink or over a drain, or you will have a major plumbing disaster.

When the plaster is dry and cool, free the castings from the molds, taking care again not to crack the castings. If you should break off a small piece, it can be glued back in place with waterproof cement or filled with wet plaster when you prepare the next batch. Cut the wire reinforcements for the next casting and proceed as before until you have six of each piece.

Trim any rough edges on the castings with a razor knife and sand any mended places with medium-grit sandpaper.

A table top fern case of Plexiglas trimmed with cast
plaster "rustic" branches and acorns. It may be used
on a glass top table as shown without its wooden base.

Paint the branches and acorns, matching as exactly as possible the natural colors of the originals. Acrylic paints work well and dry quickly. Also paint the flat backs of the branches the same color as the bark as they will show through on the inside.

When the paint is dry, spray the branches with a clear acrylic spray finish.

Spread a thin coat of waterproof glue on the backs of the branches and hold them in place on the Plexiglas with masking tape until dry. Cover the joinings of branches at the six corners and at the centers with clusters of acorns and build a finial at the peak with three large acorn halves and top it with a whole one made of two joined halves.

For a base to set the top on, cut a piece of ½" plywood the shape of your base plan adding a half an inch all around. Sand it well and paint it with dark brown or black enamel. Back it with felt to keep moisture from developing under it.

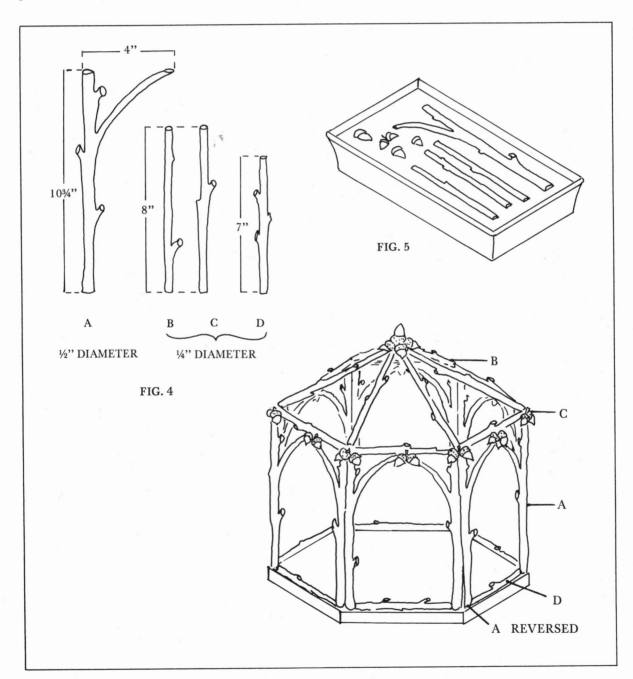

FIG. 5

A

½" DIAMETER

B   C   D

¼" DIAMETER

FIG. 4

B

C

A

D

A REVERSED

Floral Ornaments for Windows and Back Yards

These designs are still excellent ideas for anyone with limited space. The awning effect, which can be built with wire and lath, would be a pleasant addition to any window box. Even apartment dwellers with small balconies could adapt the designs for use. Different plants would create different effects. Ivy would make an almost permanent planting, while a fast-growing annual such as Heavenly Blue Morning Glory, would make an impressive show of summer color.

In our large towns the houses of the upper classes often have their windows and areas tastefully decorated with flowers and plants. The floral profusion which adorns the windows of a West End mansion is, however, purchased or hired at a large expense, and to obtain a similar result by the same means would be impossible for those whose incomes are small. But this is no reason why not only the windows but also the back yards of the homes of the lower, middle, and working classes should be barred from the inexpensive adornment of living and refreshing foliage, such as is to be produced by common climbing and creeping plants. In most Spanish towns, not only are the terraced roofs and balconies of the houses overgrown with creeping plants, but even the streets themselves are in many places festooned and overhung with this description of vegetation. There might, perhaps, be some difficulty in England in prevailing upon all the inhabitants of a narrow street, alley, or court to combine in rendering their common premises more pleasant to the sight in this manner, but we are of the opinion that there are cases in which even this could be done. . . .

Window Canopy

The illustration, Fig. 1, shows how with a few simple appliances a window may be at the same time sheltered from the sun and rendered pretty. A is a framework of a few laths nailed together, which by means of rings

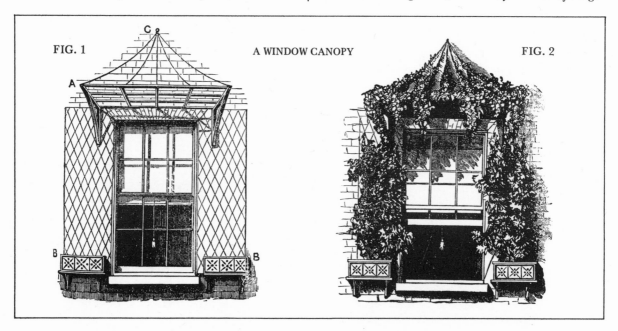

FIG. 1   A WINDOW CANOPY   FIG. 2

A TEMPORARY ARBOR

or staples at its two upper corners may be hung upon hooks, driven into the wall, during the summer, and removed before winter. Two or more brackets, B, B, are fastened on either side of the window sill, to receive flower-pots, and between these and the framework, nails are driven into the wall so that strings can be tied upon them to form a kind of lozenge-shaped trellis-work. A further improvement can be made by carrying strings, as at C, from the top of the framework to a hook driven into the wall above. In Fig. 2 we show this as it would appear when covered with evergreens. For cultivation in this instance some of the smaller climbing plants might be used, such as the canary creeper, the major convolvulus, the sweet pea &c. The above arrangement can also be adapted to a doorway.

Temporary Arbor

Where such decorations would not interfere with the uses to which back yards have often to be applied, such places may be embellished by the cultivation of creepers in various ways. The idea of a small temporary arbour in the center of the yard is taken from one we have seen on the Continent. Such an arbour is a pleasing sight from the windows and agreeable to sit within. We have shown the pots of creeping plants placed at a little distance apart, but they may, of course, be brought much closer together, or there may be two rows of them, so as, in fact to form a close wall of foliage. The construction is very simple. A piece of wood is placed across the yard from wall to wall, and from the center of this a hoop is suspended by strings; from the hoop the strings radiate downward and outward to a circle of pots placed upon the ground and containing the creepers. It will be seen that the whole of the materials required would cost the merest trifle.

A small yard may also, if desired, be roofed in during the summer time by strings drawn across the top, and run over with creepers; and covered walks and arbours of different forms may be made in this same manner, the chief outlay required being merely a little agreeable labor.

Portable Screen of Ivy

This is a very useful article for many purposes; it may be used to place before a summer-house entrance when occupied, or to conceal parts of an ugly wall, and so give greater charm to a small and monotonous plot of ground; or it can be used to hide a back door, or some ugly nook or corner, or gardener's dust-hole.

A common flower box is made the length required and mounted on castors. The size of the screen depends on the purpose for which it is wanted. A number of laths of wood as long as the screen is to be high, must be placed upright at intervals all along the box, against the back of it and resting on the bottom of it. Nail them in their places. A number more laths, as long as the box is wide, must now be fixed across these. Begin with the first an inch above the box. Fix it right across by two tacks, one at each extremity. Fix it to every lath with fine wire. Paint it green and when dry the box is filled with mould and set with ivy plants which will cover the trellis completely as they grow. The front of the box should be set thickly with lily of the valley, or scented violet roots. Lilies of the valley give a particular fragrance that is not only delightful to inhale, but which is reputed to cure headache.

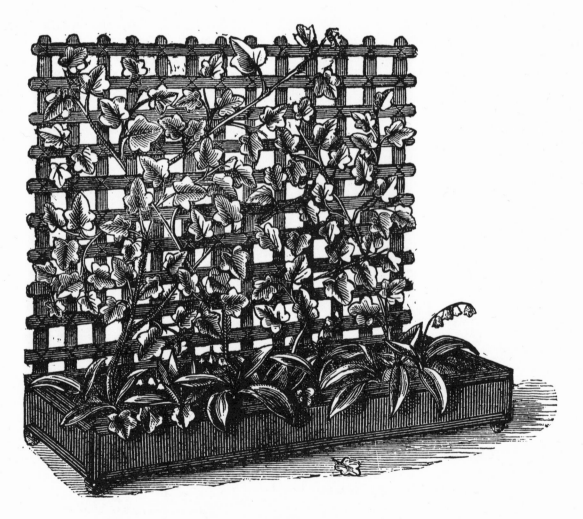

A PORTABLE SCREEN OF IVY

Tame Pigeons and Doves

Pigeons were not kept solely as pets, even though Cassell's moving description might lead one to think so. He quotes Baron Brisse, one of the "greatest authorities on French cooking, who boasts that he has at his fingers' ends not less than sixty-two ways of dressing pigeons. He gives them titles, some of which, as 'Merry Pigeons,' are amusing." Cassell sounds rather indignant when he adds that the good Baron does not have "our excellent English pigeon pie" on the list.

There are, we imagine, few persons so devoid of all sense of sympathy with their feathered fellow-creatures as to feel no interest or delight in pigeons — the ease with which they may be placed on the most intimate terms with their master, their variety and beauty of shape and plumage, the tenderness of their voices, their absurd antics and small vanities, their struttings and love-makings, all combine to render them an endless source of amusement and pleasure to every properly organised mind. No country house, or, indeed, any house where pigeons can be kept, is complete without them.

Of the keeping of fancy pigeons specially, we do not propose to treat at length. As much and perhaps more real pleasure is to be derived from the commoner kinds, and to most persons they will prove of greater profit. . . . Fancy birds are more subject to diseases than common ones, added to which some kinds of fancy birds are deficient in moral qualities, and are bad nurses of their young.

The tame pigeon, like all the wild members of the family, lays two eggs, neither less nor more, and these usually produce a male and a female. The period of incubation is seventeen days. The conjugal fidelity of all the family is proverbial, and the male bird shares the duty of sitting with the female. . . .

The young pigeon, when first hatched, is one of the most helpless little creatures (human babies always excepted) to be found in animated Nature.

For some days previous to hatching, the crops of the old birds have been filling with what pigeon-keepers call "soft-meat" which consists of partially digested food, and is analogous to the milk of mammals. The parent puts its beak within that of the young bird and throws this food into its throat. This continues for seven or eight days, then feeding with ordinary "hard-food" continues till the young are capable of picking up for themselves, at about five weeks. While fed with soft food the technical name for the young pigeon is "a squab," afterwards it is known as "a squeaker" till it reaches the full dignity of pigeonhood, and is capable of pairing, at six months. The number of broods to be reared from a pair in the year will generally be about six or seven.

If the dove-cote is a building specially raised for the purpose, the breeding holes are usually contrived in the thickness of the walls; but a good dove-cote may be constructed in the gable of a stable or other building. In this case wooden cells will be necessary. . . . Strips of wood three inches wide should run along the fronts of the shelves to prevent the eggs and the young from falling off, and on which the pigeons can alight and disport themselves, and carry on the chief amusement of pigeon life — flirtation. A dove-cote ought to be well lighted, and it should be whitewashed once every year. The tillage which it produces may be removed in November, and again at the end of February. The young of the dove-cote pigeon are reared in a nest lined by their own dung, which if left in the hole after the birds are gone is apt to harbor vermin.

Pigeons are less likely to forsake a large dove-house in which many birds are kept than a small one. Small flights frequently go off to join larger ones, but the reverse is rare. No means should be neglected of attaching the birds to their home. Pigeons are said to be fond of strong scents, such as assafoetida, and it is held a good plan to sprinkle the floor with that or some other strong odoriferous substance before stocking a dove-cote. A method much in vogue with pigeon fanciers to keep birds from straying is the "Salt Cat." Formerly a real dead cat was salted, spiced, and roasted for the purpose; upon this the modern practice is a slight improvement, but is still sufficiently disgusting; the following is an approved receipe for making it. Take half a gallon of gravel or sand, half gallon of rubbish from an old wall, a quarter pound of aniseed, a quarter pound of saltpetre, and a handful of common salt; knead into a stiff paste with stale chamber-ley, and put it into earthen vessels with holes in the sides through which the birds can peck out the compound.

Many persons will be too fastidious to use this; in that case they should provide its chief constituents, the lime and salt, in a box for the benefit of their birds.

Pigeon fanciers are not, perhaps, as a class, the most elevated in the social scale, and it is possible that many readers would not care to be included in the fraternity.

DOVECOTS

Sun Dials

At first glance, the directions for making sun dials seemed terribly complicated, but when we actually sat down with drawing tools and a protractor and worked it out step by step, it wasn't too hard at all. This would be an excellent practical project to do with youngsters in the throes of geometry.

Remember that a sun dial is exactly accurate on only four days of the year, April 15, June 15, September 1, and December 24, but the greatest variation is only sixteen minutes for several days in November.

We have printed the technical parts of Cassell's instructions in full, then described the sun dial that we made.

If the mathematics of plotting the dial still seems too complicated, we have included on page 222 a table of the angles of the hour lines for horizontal dials for latitudes from 30° N to 60° N. These angles are measured from the noon line as indicated at the top of the chart.

In the present age, when clocks are so abundant that a tolerably good one may be bought for two shillings, there would appear to be danger of the more ancient chronometer, the sun-dial, being forgotten. We should be sorry should such be the case, for it is an instrument which has long done good service to man. . . . Making dials forms an interesting amusement, affording scope for both thought and taste, and has occupied the leisure hours of many eminent men. We believe that many of our readers will be glad of a few plain directions on its construction. . . . We propose to treat only of the more simple ones, which are best adapted for use upon a pedestal in the garden; and are so easily made as to be within reach of the capacity of every person.

The theory of dialing we should find difficult to explain fully without the use of dia-

grams and a long scientific dissertation; we shall, therefore briefly say that the horizontal dial represents the plane of the horizon while, the gnomen, which casts the shadow, represents the axis of the earth. This, therefore, must be more or less inclined to the dial, as the place for which the dial is intended is nearer to or further from the equator; hence, before making a dial, it will be necessary to ascertain the latitude of the place. From a terrestrial globe this can at once be learnt by anyone who understands the use of such an instrument; or, which is much easier, the latitude of a place, or that of a town sufficiently near for all practical purposes can be found in the index appended to most atlases.

The horizontal dial is usually engraved on a plate of metal or a slab of stone or slate. The latter will probably be preferred by the amateur diallist, since it is always readily procurable, and the lines and figures may easily be cut in it even with the point of a knife; and it also stands weather well, and is generally suitable for the purpose. The gnomen, by which the shadow is cast to point the hour, is better made of metal, brass being best; but in situations where there is no danger of breakage, slate may be used for this purpose also.

To draw a horizontal dial, take a piece of paper, as in Fig. 1, of the size of the proposed dial, and through the center draw a meridian line, AB, which will represent the 12 o'clock line. At somewhat more than one-third from the end of this and cutting it at G, draw a second line at right angles to it, CD: this line will represent 6 o'clock. On the line CD, from any point — as say at E — draw the line EF, forming with EG an angle, which will be equal to the latitude of the place for which the sun-dial is intended. From the center of the line, EF, draw a perpendicular equal to half its length, as HI; and from I draw lines to E and F. Then, with the compasses, with

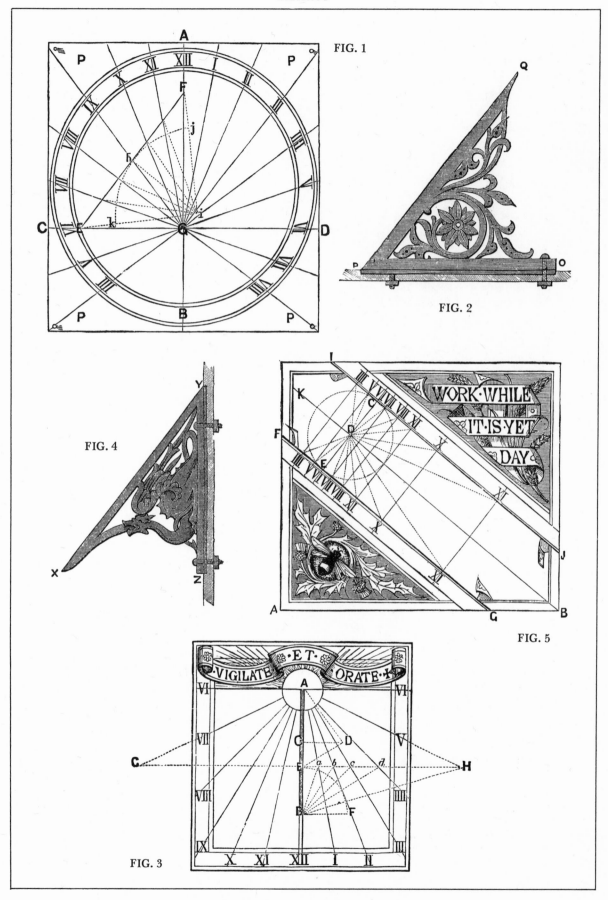

FIG. 1

FIG. 2

FIG. 4

WORK·WHILE
IT·IS·YET
DAY

FIG. 5

·ET·
VIGILATE ORATE·

FIG. 3

218

I as a center, draw the quadrant, JK, and divide this into six equal parts, and, through the points thus gained, draw lines from G to the edge of the paper, as before; these will give the hour lines from 6 AM to 12 noon. Halves and quarters must be obtained in the same manner as the hours. The afternoon hours from 12 to 6, may be obtained by simply folding the paper on the line AB, and tracing through as the two sides will correspond exactly. To obtain the early morning hours 4 and 5, and the evening hours 7 and 8, we have merely to continue the morning hours 7 and 8, and the evening hours 4 and 5, through the point G to the opposite edge of the paper.

Generally speaking, for a horizontal dial a circular form is preferred; but before circumscribing the dial with a circular line, it will be necessary to cut the paper into two pieces through the line AB; these should be pinned down with just so much space between them as will be equal to the thickness of the gnomen. Then take the compasses, and from about the middle of the paper strike a circle, within which figures indicating the hours may be marked, as shown in the diagram, and from this paper the necessary lines and figures may be traced off upon the actual dial, in which they should be accurately engraved.

The gnomen must be of triangular shape (see Fig. 2), having the angle P equal to the angle E, in Fig. 1, or, in other words, equal to as many degrees as the latitude of the place. In fixing the gnomen, the angle P, Fig. 2, will fall upon the point G, Fig. 1, and O upon the meridian line toward F. The line PQ on the face of the gnomen must always be left perfectly strong, as it is by the shadow thrown by this line that time will be indicated, but the under parts may be cut away in any ornamental form that may be preferred. The top of the pedestal on which this dial is to be placed must be perfectly horizontal; and the 12 o'clock line or that occupied by the gnomen, just run due north and south.

The pedestal of the horizontal dial affords great scope for the display of taste, if carving or modeling be employed, or a pretty pedes-

tal may be made of the rough stump of a tree, with creepers twined round it. And here we would suggest that a great mistake is frequently committed in making the pedestals of horizontal dials too high. A pedestal of not more than three and a half feet above the ground allows the time to be seen with much greater readiness, and is, therefore, better adapted for the purpose than the more lofty one.

The dial itself may be a conspicuous and highly ornamental feature. Symbols emblematical of time are always appropriate. We have seen one, of which a mediaeval ship (an emblem of the course of time) formed the base, the meridian line the mast, the hourlines the cordage; and with our ancestors, appropriate mottoes, such as furnish food for wholesome reflections, were also favorite methods of decoration. We quote the following from old dials; they were generally in Latin, owing to its greater terseness. Thus at Gloucester, we have "Pereunt et imputantur" (They pass away, and are placed to our account); at Mickelton, "Noli confidere nocti" (Trust not the night), which suggests the text, "The night cometh, when no man can work," which would, in itself, be a good motto; or "Lex Dei lux diei" (The law of God is the light of day); at Packwood, in Warwickshire, "Orimur, morimur" (We are born, we die); and at Rouen, one which puzzles some few tourists, "Ultimam time" (Fear the last hour); at Bridgend, "Fugit irreparabile tempus" (Irredeemable time flies away); at Warwick, "Vigliate et orate" (Watch and pray); at Maidstone, "Umbra sumus" (We are a shadow); and in London was one which said to the idler, "Begone about your business."

Figs. 1 and 2 are for the horizontal dial; Figs. 3, 4 and 5 are for vertical dials and included to show decorative motifs.

Carved Redwood Horizontal Sun Dial

This brass-and-redwood sun dial was really very easy to make and the results are most attractive. We used linoleum carving tools, which are quite inexpensive, and they were more than adequate for the soft redwood.

You will need:

Clear, dry fine-grained redwood 12" square and 2" thick
Brass strips, 5 feet of 32 mil and ¼" wide
Brass, 4" by 10" sheet of 32 mil
Clear acrylic spray finish
Wood or linoleum carving tools
Fine-toothed hack saw or jeweler's saw
Compass, T square, triangle, and protractor
Medium and fine sandpaper
Cardboard
Tracing paper
Razor knife
Rattail file
Plastic wood
Fine emery paper

Enlarge the drawing of the dial to twice the size shown. This may be done by drawing a grid of 1" squares as shown in the broken lines. Notice that there is an additional ¼" on two sides. Now sketch in the outlines in the corresponding squares.

Plot the hour lines on a piece of tracing paper, using Cassell's directions or the angles given for your latitude on the chard (see 222). Cut a cardboard gnomen and set up a model dial to test your calculations before starting to carve.

Sand your wood well and transfer the design, with the exception of the hour lines, onto the block. When carving, make deep cuts with the razor knife outlining the portions of the design which are to be left raised and then carving away the background (shown shaded in the drawing). If you do not outline your design carefully, you will find that the wood will split along the grain and spoil the design.

When the carving is complete, transfer the hour lines onto the dial face. Measure the ¼" brass to the lengths of the lines — except the twelve o'clock line — and cut with a hack saw. Sand the ends until smooth.

With a sharp razor knife, make a light cut along the horizontal hour line, being care-ful to keep it accurate. Go over the cut several times until you are sure it is at least ¼" deep. Do not try to make it that deep in one cut. Keep the edges of the cut sharp and clean. Press one end of the brass into the cut and tap it gently into the wood with a hammer. Now move slowly up the strip, tapping it into the groove. Be careful not to hit the face of the dial. When the entire strip is securely into the groove, go back to the beginning and hammer it deeper, moving slowly along the brass strip. At this point, it is wiser to use a small flat piece of wood between the hammer and the brass to prevent bending the brass or denting the face. Continue to hammer until the strip is flush with the surface of the dial.

Now make your next cut and insert the brass in the same manner. Cut only one hour line at a time or you will split away the wood at the center of the dial. If you should split away a large piece, glue it back in place with white glue; small chips can be repaired in the finishing process.

When all of the brass pieces are as nearly flush as you can make them, fill any chips or gaps with redwood-colored plastic wood. When dry, sand the face with medium grit sandpaper, working with the grain of the wood, until the wood and brass are perfectly smooth and even. Finish off with fine sandpaper.

Draw a paper pattern of your gnomen. Ours is a very simple shape. Remember to leave enough width on the bottom to embed in the wooden face, approximately 1/4" to 5/8". Trace the outline on to the sheet of brass and cut it out with a hack saw or jeweler's saw. If you are using a hack saw, you will not be able to cut a smooth curve and it will need further shaping with a rattail file. Sand the edges and faces with fine emery paper.

Cut a groove for the gnomen along the twelve o'clock line and gently tap it into place making sure to keep it at right angles to the face.

Finish it with several coats of clear acrylic spray.

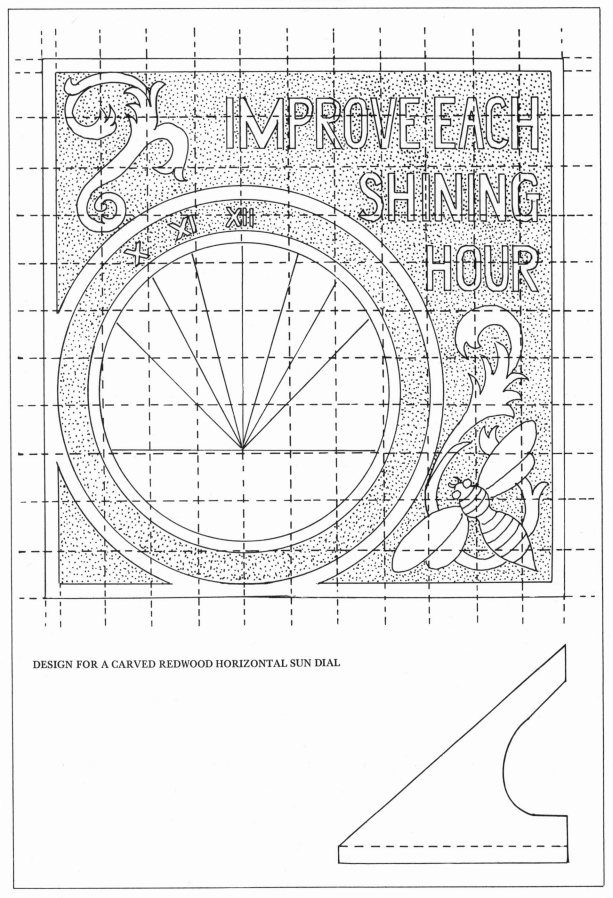

DESIGN FOR A CARVED REDWOOD HORIZONTAL SUN DIAL

Table of Hour Line Angles According
to Latitudes in the Northern Hemisphere

Latitude (North).	12	11 12 1	10 12 2	9 12 3	8 12 4	7 12 5	12 / 6 6
30°	0°00	7°38′	16°06′	26°34′	40°54′	61°49′	90°00′
31	0 00	7 52	16 34	27 15	41 44	62 31	90 00
32	0 00	8 05	17 01	27 55	42 33	63 11	90 00
33	0 00	8 18	17 27	28 35	43 20	63 48	90 00
34	0 00	8 31	17 54	29 13	44 05	64 24	90 00
35	0 00	8 44	18 19	29 50	44 49	64 58	90 00
36	0 00	8 57	18 45	30 27	45 31	65 29	90 00
37	0 00	9 10	19 10	31 03	46 12	66 00	90 00
38	0 00	9 22	19 34	31 37	46 50	66 29	90 00
39	0 00	9 34	19 58	32 11	47 28	66 56	90 00
40	0 00	9 46	20 22	32 44	48 04	67 22	90 00
41	0 00	9 58	20 45	33 16	48 39	67 47	90 00
42	0 00	10 10	21 07	33 47	49 13	68 11	90 00
43	0 00	10 21	21 29	34 18	49 45	68 33	90 00
44	0 00	10 33	21 51	34 47	50 16	68 55	90 00
45	0 00	10 44	22 12	35 16	50 46	69 15	90 00
46	0 00	10 55	22 33	35 42	51 15	69 34	90 00
47	0 00	11 05	22 53	36 11	51 43	69 53	90 00
48	0 00	11 16	23 13	36 37	52 10	70 10	90 00
49	0 00	11 26	23 33	37 03	52 35	70 27	90 00
50	0 00	11 36	23 51	37 27	53 00	70 43	90 00
51	0 00	11 46	24 10	37 51	53 24	70 59	90 00
52	0 00	11 55	24 28	38 14	53 46	71 13	90 00
53	0 00	12 05	24 45	38 37	54 09	71 28	90 00
54	0 00	12 14	25 02	38 59	54 30	71 41	90 00
55	0 00	12 23	25 19	39 20	54 50	71 53	90 00
56	0 00	12 31	25 35	39 40	55 09	72 06	90 00
57	0 00	12 40	25 50	39 59	55 28	72 17	90 00
58	0 00	12 48	26 05	40 18	55 45	72 28	90 00
59	0 00	13 00	26 20	40 36	56 03	72 39	90 00
60	0 00	13 04	26 34	40 53	56 19	72 49	90 00

. . . and our special appreciation
to Queen Victoria
without whose contribution
none of this could have happened.